IMAGES
of America

The SHAKER COMMUNITIES
of KENTUCKY
Pleasant Hill and South Union

Love Ya,

Art & Carol

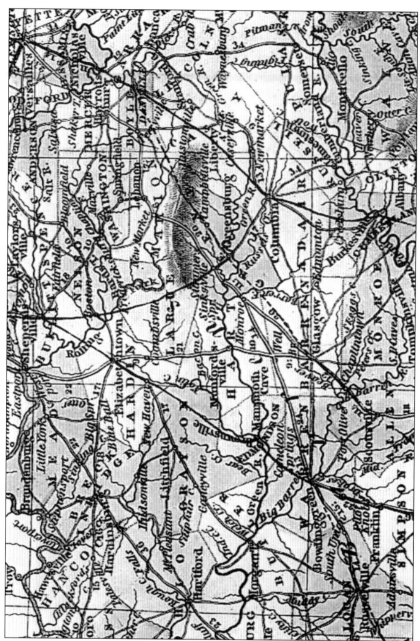

SEGMENT OF 1850 KENTUCKY MAP. This map segment is from "A New Map of Kentucky with its Roads and Distances along the Stage and Steam Boat Routes. Published by Thomas, Cowperthwait & Co.," 1850. Pleasant Hill is shown as "Shaker T." (for Shaker Town) in the northeast corner of the segment (southwest of Lexington). South Union is in the southwest corner, in Logan County. The distance between the villages was about 130 miles. (Courtesy of United States Digital Map Library, USGenWeb Archives, http://www.rootsweb.com/~usgenweb/maps/.)

ON THE COVER: The 1810 Building at South Union stood for well over a century, first serving as a dwelling; for many years it was used as the community's schoolhouse. (Courtesy of Western Reserve Historical Society.)

IMAGES
of America

The SHAKER COMMUNITIES
of KENTUCKY
Pleasant Hill and South Union

James W. Hooper
Forewords by Larrie Curry of Pleasant Hill
and Tommy Hines of South Union

ARCADIA
PUBLISHING

Published by Arcadia Publishing
Charleston SC, Chicago IL, Portsmouth NH, San Francisco CA

Printed in the United States of America

Library of Congress Catalog Card Number: 2006920984

For all general information contact Arcadia Publishing at:
Telephone 843-853-2070
Fax 843-853-0044
E-mail sales@arcadiapublishing.com
For customer service and orders:
Toll-Free 1-888-313-2665

Visit us on the Internet at www.arcadiapublishing.com

For my wife, Mona Nading Hooper—devoted wife, mother, grandmother, friend, registered nurse—with love, appreciation, and admiration.

PLEASANT HILL 1834 CENTRE HOUSE. Among the most impressive buildings in all the Shaker villages, this beautiful building was home to many busy Shaker sisters and brethren. It sits on the main road through the village. (Courtesy of Library of Congress, Prints and Photographs Division, Historic American Buildings Survey [HABS].)

CONTENTS

Preface   6

Foreword by Larrie Curry   7

Foreword by Tommy Hines   8

Introduction   9

1. Shaker Beginnings   11

2. Shakers in America   17

3. The Second Great Awakening   23

4. Shaker Converts in Kentucky   31

5. Villages and Farms   37

6. Beliefs and Worship   63

7. Busy Lives   73

8. Interaction with the World   87

9. Difficulties and Decline   97

10. Pleasant Hill and South Union Today   125

Bibliography   128

PREFACE

A long-term casual interest in the Shakers transitioned to a deeper interest during 2002 when, as part of my Marshall University sabbatical leave, my wife, Mona, and I visited a number of the historical Shaker sites in Kentucky, Ohio, New York, and New England. The focus of the sabbatical was to examine the climate for innovation characterizing the Shaker communities and draw applicable inferences. I subsequently presented papers at international conferences on engineering management, technology management, and business and economic history, analyzing Shaker culture and organization as a means to account for their originality and innovativeness and their success in conducting business with "the world."

My first interview during the sabbatical was with Tommy Hines, executive director of the Shaker Museum at South Union. Since that time, he has been an unfailing source of encouragement and support. After my recent retirement from Marshall University, I undertook this book project, with Tommy encouraging it even before I began it. I am very grateful to him. I also owe a debt of gratitude to Larrie Curry, who is vice president and museum director of the Shaker Village of Pleasant Hill. She has been generous to share her time, knowledge, and resources. I very much appreciate Tommy and Larrie contributing forewords for the book, reading drafts of the chapters and image captions, and offering helpful suggestions. They and their respective organizations have graciously permitted use of many vintage images that appear in this book.

Thanks to numerous others who have been helpful in providing access to images and permission for use. Thanks to Lauren Bobier of Arcadia Publishing, who has been helpful and encouraging throughout this project.

James W. Hooper
February 2006

FOREWORD
BY LARRIE CURRY

The physical presence of the Kentucky Shakers survives in the fine buildings; well-built, sometimes elegant, furniture; objects of daily life; and an extraordinary body of manuscript material and music. All of these are evidence of the principles guiding Shaker life, as these dedicated people endeavored to create a temporal existence in tune with their spiritual world.

The Shaker Village of Pleasant Hill stands as a living testament to the remarkable society and the ordinary people who accepted the challenge to pursue paradise. Pleasant Hill today is also a monument to the vision and persistence of many dedicated individuals who brought the village back from the brink of ruin in the mid-1960s and continue to care for the rich heritage of its builders.

Thirty-four historic structures, 20 miles of rock fences, and 2,900 acres of rolling countryside, once tilled by Pleasant Hill Shakers, are shared with thousands of visitors annually. Programs focus on telling the story of the people who lived here and how that story is relevant to us today.

It has been many years since we have seen such a collection of historical images of those who peopled the streets, dwellings, and shops of Pleasant Hill and South Union. Not since the publication of Julia Neal's *The Kentucky Shakers* has a work focused on the importance of the two Kentucky Shaker communities, their kinship with each other and the larger Shaker society, as well as the distinctly regional character of the southernmost Shaker villages.

James W. Hooper's book captures the beginnings, building, and flourishing of the Kentucky Shaker communities. It also tells of the difficulties of perpetuating the brave experiment into the 20th century. Dr. Hooper's work honors the achievements of the Kentucky Shakers, who strove for perfection, were completely human, but remained faithful to their ideal.

Larrie Spier Curry
Vice President and Museum Director
Shaker Village of Pleasant Hill
February 2006

FOREWORD
BY TOMMY HINES

The process of piecing together the history of South Union continues to fascinate researchers because of a seemingly endless supply of original manuscript records. These carefully preserved journals, letters, ledgers, and diaries penned by the Shakers between 1807 and 1922 are invaluable written reminders of a culture that came to an end in Kentucky over 80 years ago. Yet without photographs, the manuscripts alone only allow the reader to imagine what South Union and its inhabitants might have looked like.

Historic photographs let us actually see what our minds only visualize from the written word. In the case of South Union, where so much of the built environment has been destroyed, photographs become a priceless component of its history. Only 9 of 225 structures built within the confines of the village remain, and unfortunately, historic photographs of South Union are rare.

The earliest known photographs made in the community date from around 1885. This set of large-format cabinet cards shot by a professional photographer are now in the collection of the Western Reserve Historical Society in Cleveland, Ohio. Because the cabinet cards were numbered on the original glass negatives and because there are gaps in the numbers, we know that the entire set has not surfaced. What survives, however, are beautifully composed shots of South Union at its final peak, just as the community was beginning its slow, almost 40-year decline. No indication of that decline is visible in these fine photographs, several of which are included in this book.

Professional photographs were not made again until the spring of 1922, when the auction company handling South Union's dissolution shot a series of pictures for the auction catalog. The structures look to be in an excellent state of preservation, a testament to the Shakers' efforts to maintain the village at a time when money was scarce and the labor force long gone. These 8-by-10-inch double weight photographs are crystal clear, revealing wonderful detail in two interior shots and five exterior views.

The remainder of South Union's historic photograph collection, with only a few exceptions, is made up of studio cabinet card portraits of members who visited photographers outside the village and photographs made by amateurs who visited South Union. While most of these shots focus on carefully posed "world's people," one can also gain rare glimpses of Shaker buildings not captured elsewhere.

Unlike many of the other Shaker villages, there were no stereoviews of South Union and only one known postcard produced for circulation, and it was incorrectly attributed to Pleasant Hill. Additionally most of the candid photographs made at the beginning of the 20th century were shot around or near the Centre Family buildings. As the result, only about 30 of South Union's buildings are documented through photography.

This wonderful collection of photographs, both historic and contemporary, marks the first time a book of images from both of Kentucky's Shaker villages has been published. Dr. Hooper's thorough research and affection for the subject are evident in the pages that follow. I am confident that the book will pique the interest of scholars who are seeing many of these photographs for the first time. For those who simply have a desire to know more about the Shakers' Kentucky adventure, I hope this book will stimulate an even greater appreciation.

Tommy Hines
Executive Director
Shaker Museum at South Union
February 23, 2006

INTRODUCTION

Along U.S. Highway 68 in Kentucky are two historical villages that were for many years home to Kentucky's Shakers. Pleasant Hill, near Harrodsburg, and South Union, near Bowling Green, provide silent testimony about the remarkable people who lived there. The buildings are simple but beautiful and exceptionally well constructed, as their endurance testifies. The plans of the villages reflect religious commitment, with a meetinghouse as the central focus. The internal designs of the large dwelling houses accommodate communal living and celibacy—two basic tenets of the Shakers. The numerous artifacts on display in the villages bespeak an attention to detail and quality characteristic of people who were, in the words of Shaker leader Ann Lee, to "put your hands to work, and give your hearts to God."

Each year, thousands of people visit the Shaker villages in Kentucky and other states, and interest in the Shakers continues to grow. The contrast of Shaker lives to our own is striking and interesting to many of us. Their religious and lifestyle practices—especially celibacy—bring about a great deal of curiosity. The simple pattern and structure of their lives, so very different from our own, has a certain appeal. There is also great interest in their elegantly simple furniture and other items. Whatever the appeal may be, more and more of us are visiting the villages, reading about the Shakers, and buying Shaker furniture—originals and reproductions.

The Shakers were committed to serve God and live a life apart from "the world" but were always interested in labor-saving methods and devices. They readily accepted inventions from the world, frequently improving on them and devising inventions of their own. It surprises many to learn this about the Shakers, the assumption being that they were perhaps somewhat like the "old order" Amish of our day who reject recent innovations. Nothing could be further from the truth, as we will see.

Kentucky Shakers were in many ways similar to their eastern Shaker brethren but different in some ways, too. They were given to doing things "their way," sometimes to the consternation of their "headquarters" in New York, and of course had regional emphasis in their farming and industrial endeavors. As we will see, however, they were every bit as committed, creative, hardworking, and successful as Shakers of other regions. The Shaker experience in Kentucky had its beginnings in the early 19th century, a time of great religious revival in the region. The religious seeking of the time provided fertile ground for Shaker doctrine and also led to the beginnings of several other religious movements that are still active in our time.

By means of images and explanatory text, this book provides perspective about the Kentucky Shakers—their motivations, their successes, and their failures. Insights include why it was that some people in Kentucky accepted a radical religious doctrine that included celibacy as a tenet, giving up their families and possessions to live in a communal arrangement with other believers, why they were so successful for so long, and how close they came to achieving their utopian goals in their lives and relationships. Insights are provided as to whether celibacy was the reason for the eventual demise of the Shaker villages, as is commonly thought, or whether there were other causes. Although they turned their backs on the world, they surpassed their neighbors in the comfort and productivity of their villages and farms. How was it that they could live in substantial homes when many of their neighbors lived in log cabins? Was there a conflict between their commitment to a simple life and separateness from the world, with their surprising inventiveness and their extensive interaction with the world? How were they perceived by their neighbors? How different were their daily lives from those of their neighbors? We consider these questions in the following chapters.

This book examines and depicts Shaker beliefs and worship, their spiritual and temporal organization, their relationships with each other and the world, their work assignments, and their human struggles. Fortunately the Shakers kept daily records of much that occurred in their lives, including small details of daily life as well as matters of greater import. Some of the Shakers wrote about their beliefs and practices in order to explain themselves to the world. Contemporary non-Shakers visited Shaker villages and wrote about their impressions. Much of this material has been carefully preserved.

The Shakers of Kentucky and other states have left a legacy worthy of our consideration. Their beliefs pervaded every aspect of their lives, governing their relationships with God, their leaders, other believers, and the world, and their attitudes and efforts in their work. They manifestly had failings as an organization, from the Shaker viewpoint, given that there are no Shakers in Kentucky today. But they had many notable successes in their day. We stand to benefit from an understanding of this remarkable people of an earlier time.

One

SHAKER BEGINNINGS

Ann Lee was a principal leader of the religious group that came to be known as Shakers. She was one of eight children of a poor blacksmith who lived on Toad Lane in the slums of Manchester, England. Her birth date is uncertain, but according to Shaker traditions, she was born in 1736. There is a record of her baptism in the cathedral on June 1, 1742. When she was very young, she began working in a cotton factory and had no formal schooling. In 1758, while she was still unmarried, Ann and her parents joined a sect led by James and Jane Wardley, who were considered by their followers to be a prophet and prophetess. They were influenced by the beliefs of the Quakers and by the French Prophets (or Camisards)—who claimed divine guidance and gifts of prophecy and who were characterized in worship by suddenly falling backward and undergoing involuntary contortions. The group came to be called "Shaking Quakers," or just Shakers, due to the ecstatic "fits" they experienced during worship, with shouting, trembling, singing, and dancing. They were said to end each gathering only when they became exhausted.

The sect met frequently in the homes of members for worship, and the noise of their worship was disturbing to residents at some distance from the meeting place. By 1772, they began the extreme tactic of disrupting worship services of churches in the area in order to call attention to their teaching. This resulted in arrests, jail time, and fines for Ann, her father, John Lees, and others. The sect's tactics also resulted in confrontations with neighbors, requiring intervention by a constable to disperse mobs. Her arrests reflect the increasingly important role she was playing among the Shakers.

Ann Lees (later shortened to Lee) was married in 1762 to Abraham Standerin (sometimes called Stanley or Standley), a blacksmith. Perhaps this resulted from family pressure, or as Shaker history indicates, she had not yet "attained to that knowledge of God which she so early desired." She gave birth to four children, all of whom died in infancy. This sad experience evidently strengthened her conviction that the "lustful gratifications of the flesh" were the basis of human depravity. The Shaker group came to accept that "cohabitation of the sexes" was a major source of evil. Reportedly Ann Lees received "a special manifestation of Divine light," causing the small group of believers to accept her as "Mother in Christ" and leader of the Shakers.

Numerous accounts were given by her followers of her ability to discern the true character and hidden lives of individuals. She was known to directly confront visitors about their sinful nature and implore them to confess their sins and become adherents to the Shaker testimony. She also admonished believers to strive for perfection. She taught numerous maxims to her followers, such as "put your hands to work, and give your hearts to God; for if you are not faithful in the unrighteous mammon, how can you expect the true riches?" and "do all your work as though you had a thousand years to live, and as you would if you knew you must die tomorrow."

Ann Lee was thought by her followers to be the "second embodiment of the Christ Spirit" and that she represented the female nature of God. Shaker teachings made women fully equal with men. The following description was included in the Shaker publication *A Summary View of the Millennial Church* (Green and Wells 1823):

> Mother Ann Lee, in her personal appearance, was a woman rather below the common stature of woman; thick set, but straight and other wise well proportioned and regular in form and features. Her complexion was light and fair, and her eyes were blue, but keen and penetrating. . . . Her manners were plain, simple and easy; yet she possessed a certain dignity of appearance that inspired confidence and commanded respect. By many of the world, who saw her without prejudice, she was called beautiful; and to her faithful children, she appeared to possess a degree of dignified beauty and heavenly love, which they had never before discovered among mortals.

Being illiterate herself, Lee rejected written creeds and statements of belief. She and her followers considered revelation as dynamic and changing, valuing the spoken word as more accommodating. Eventually the Shakers began to write in their own defense and undertook to document events long past by relying on "remembrance by a special gift of God." Not surprisingly, the credibility of these documents has been challenged by historians. The official name of the movement came to be the United Society of Believers in Christ's Second Appearing, but they were usually known as Shakers, and the name originally applied in derision by the world eventually was used by the believers.

In 1774, Lees and a small group of Shakers decided to relocate to America. The decision was apparently influenced by the limited success of their efforts in Manchester, their increasing legal difficulties, and the hope of better circumstances in America. Ann saw visions of a chosen people in New England, and James Whittaker, a member of the group, had a vision of the church in America as a large tree, which "shone with such brightness, as made it appear like a burning torch." In the spring of 1774, Ann Lees sailed from Liverpool for New York with her husband, her brother William, James Whittaker, and five other religious adherents.

John Son of James Evans Grazier
Betty Dau of John Hodgin weaver
Betty Dau of Geo: & Ann Lees of M
Peter Son of Peter Hough Carpent
John Son of Willm Poole —

Christeings in June
Ann daur to John Lee was privately baptisd
Robt Son of Henry Hindley Mercer
Willm Son of Jonathan Smith Brick
John Son of Isaac & Susan Clayton
Betty Dau of Ann Brownhill & Tho: A
Robt Son of Tho: Hobson Milner
John Son of James & Eliz: Wells
Marg^t Dau of John Goodyer Calend
Betty Dau of George Hilton

ANN LEE'S CHRISTENING. The baptism entry for Ann Lees, dated June 1, 1742, is shown as it appears in the Registers of Manchester Cathedral (then Manchester Collegiate Church). An explanation by Christopher Hunwick, cathedral archivist, states: "The baptism entry is irregular, as the baptism was carried out privately. The Parish Clerk had obviously already filled in the entries for the 6th June 1742, when a note was handed to him advising him of this private baptism on the 1st June. The entry is therefore squeezed in between the heading for 'June' and the first entries in June for the 6th. The father's occupation is not given." (Courtesy of Dean and Canons of Manchester Cathedral.)

Weaver ————————— and _Hannah Smethurst_ of the

No 6

Parifh _and Township of Fallowfield_ Spinster we

Married in this _Church_ by _Banns_ th

fifth ———— Day of _January_ ———— in the Year One Thousand Sev

Hundred and _Sixty two_ ———— by me _Maurice Griffith_

This Marriage was folemnized between Us {

Thomas Heywood

Hannah + Smethurst mark

In the Prefence of _Richard Dixon_

Thō: Hulme

_____

ns of Marriage _Abraham Standerin and Ann Lees were_

Published on Sunday Dec. 20th 27th and January 3d 1762 the said

Abraham Standerin ———— of this Parifh _and Town of Manchester_

No 7

———— _Blacksmith_ ———— and _Ann Lees_ ———— of the

Parifh _and Town of Manchester_ Spinster we

Married in this _Church_ by _Banns_ th

fifth ———— Day of _January_ ———— in the Year One Thousand Sev

Hundred and _Sixty One_ ———— by me _Maurice Griffith_

This Marriage was folemnized between Us {

abraham + Standerin; mark

ann + Lees; mark

In the Prefence of _James Shepperd_

Thō: Hulme

ANN LEE'S MARRIAGE RECORD. The "Banns of Marriage" for Ann Lee is dated January 5, 1761 (but should read 1762), and is signed by her and husband, Abraham Standerin, with an "X." He is listed as a blacksmith. The marriage was performed at the Manchester Collegiate Church, which became the Cathedral Church in 1847 upon creation of the Anglican Diocese of Manchester. This image is from the cathedral register. Christopher Hunwick, cathedral archivist, noted that the clerk's error is a common one near the beginning of January. (Courtesy of Dean and Canons of Manchester Cathedral.)

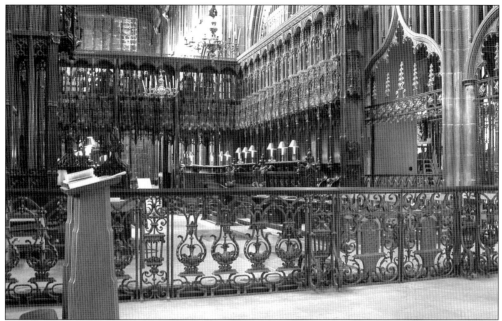

MANCHESTER CATHEDRAL. These images show scenes from Manchester Cathedral, the setting of Ann Lee's marriage. The image above is described by Christopher Hunwick, cathedral archivist: "a photograph taken from the High Altar looking west. You can see the mediaeval quire, which is unchanged since 1506, but in the foreground is the Iron work of the Altar Rail and parclose screens which were put in in 1750–1751 during Ann Lee's time at Manchester, and in front of which she would have knelt to be married. The iron work was one of the first signs of the Gothic Revival in Manchester, the gift of Samuel Baldwin Esquire." The image below is also described by Hunwick: "looking east towards the High Altar with the Lady Chapel in the background, and the ironwork rail in the foreground." (Courtesy of Dean and Canons of Manchester Cathedral.)

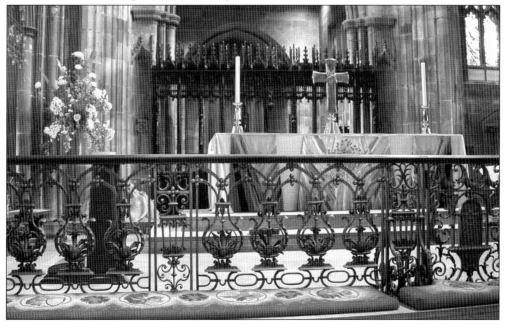

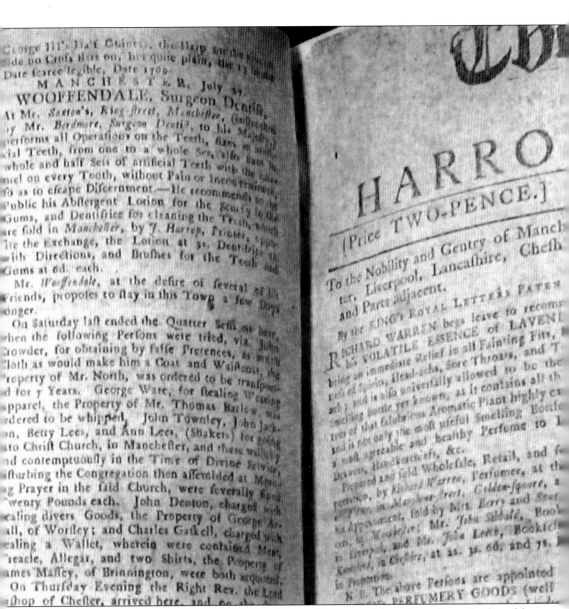

ACCOUNT OF ANN LEE'S ARREST. One of several arrests of Ann Lees (later Lee) and her associates was reported in the *Manchester Mercury* of July 27, 1773. The summary appears about two-thirds of the way down the left-hand side and states, "John Townley, John Jackson, Betty Lees, and Ann Lees, (Shakers) for going into Christ Church, in Manchester, and there willfully and contemptuously in the Time of Divine Service, disturbing the Congregation then assembled at Morning Prayer in the said Church, were severally fined Twenty Pounds each." Betty Lees was a relative of Ann Lees's father. (Courtesy of Dean and Canons of Manchester Cathedral.)

Two

SHAKERS IN AMERICA

After they arrived in America, Ann Lee and her followers scattered to different locations to earn a living and for a time held no public meetings. Little can be found in contemporary public records about their early days in America. One remaining account, which appeared in the *Boston Gazette* in November 1778, described their "dancing in extravagant postures," whirling with great rapidity, and eventually falling lifeless to the floor (Stein 1992). Ann Lee's husband soon left due to her insistence on celibacy. Several other relatives of the first group came later, and by 1779, they settled in a region called Niskeyuna, later called Watervliet, and now adjacent to the Albany (New York) International Airport. Lee (shortened from Lees after coming to America) and her companions cleared land and began providing for themselves.

The first Shakers arrived in America at a very active time religiously and politically. The Revolutionary War began in 1775, one year after their arrival, and ended in 1783. In the 1740s, the Great Awakening began in New England, with "new light" or "separatist" converts being taught to cast aside tradition and allegiance to established churches with their creeds and doctrines. There was an expectation among many that the beginning of the millennium was near, which was favorable to the Shaker teaching that the millennium had begun with them. In 1780, at New Lebanon, New York, a religious revival occurred. Some of the participants heard about Ann Lee and visited her. Visitors included Joseph Meacham, an elder among the New Light Baptists, who encouraged others to investigate her teachings. This led to converts in the vicinity of New Lebanon and nearby areas in Massachusetts and Connecticut.

Due to her encouragement of pacifism—a Quaker tenet carried over to the Shakers—charges were brought that she and her followers were opposing the revolutionary efforts of the colonies. Although it seems she did not actively take sides in the conflict, she, her brother William Lee, and John Partington were arrested and spent time in prison. In May 1781, "Mother Ann" and others began a missionary tour to visit the new converts and preach to others, and they did not return to Niskeyuna until September 1783. They encountered strong opposition at times, including beatings at Harvard, Massachusetts, but by the end of the tour, she had enough followers in various locations to form the basis for future villages. In 1781, Ezra Stiles, president of Yale College, noted in his diary that the Shakers had over 400 converts (Brewer 1986).

In July 1784, William Lee died, followed by the death of Ann Lee in September 1784 (at the age of 48, if 1736 was the year of her birth). The cause of her death is uncertain. According to Shaker traditions, she anticipated her death and shortly before she died told her followers gathered around her, "I see Brother William coming, in a golden chariot, to take me home."

Lee was succeeded in leadership by James Whittaker ("Father James"). He was literate, reading from the scriptures during worship and communicating in writing with believers in various locations. He was known for strong public defense of Shaker teachings, severe rebuke for lax followers, and condemnation of nonbelievers. He died in 1787, bringing to a close the short era of the original founders. There was as yet no formal organization and no well-defined theology. The next two principal leaders, Joseph Meacham and Lucy Wright, would address these issues. All succeeding leaders supported certain major tenets of "gospel order," namely celibacy, communalism, separation from the world, confession of sins, pacifism, and unquestioned obedience to anointed leaders.

By the end of 1787, Joseph Meacham emerged as the successor to James Whittaker. Then 45 years of age, he had considerable leadership and speaking experience. Ann Lee was quoted as saying, "Joseph Meacham is my first born son in America. He will gather the Church in order, but I shall not live to see it." An able, practical man, "Father Joseph" began to establish gospel order, putting in place a four-tiered hierarchical organization that would serve for more than 200 years. The structure consisted of a self-perpetuating central ministry at New Lebanon, bishoprics overseeing a group of regional villages, the individual villages, and families within each village. Among Meacham's assistants, the most notable was Lucy Wright, a former close associate of Ann Lee. Meacham re-introduced female leadership by appointing her as his co-equal in the ministry.

Meacham's choice of New Lebanon rather than Niskeyuna made travel more convenient between "the headquarters" and the various Shaker sites in New England. James Whittaker had a meetinghouse built on the side of the mountain above New Lebanon during his time, and Meacham gradually brought about the erection of dwelling houses and shops, creating a Shaker village on the property. During Meacham's time, 11 societies were formed by "gathering" the earlier converts. In addition to Watervliet and New Lebanon, New York, they were: Hancock, Harvard, Shirley, and Tyringham, Massachusetts; Canterbury and Enfield, New Hampshire; Alfred and Sabbathday Lake, Maine; and Enfield, Connecticut. Meacham put into place rules for entry into membership and direction for Shaker life in the new villages. In the beginning of the gathering process, new members entered into an oral covenant, but beginning in 1795, a written covenant came into use. Meacham also began to formalize theology and worship, moving away from the spontaneity in worship of earlier days. His 1790 brochure entitled *Concise Statement of the Only True Church* was the first written document defining Shaker faith and practice.

Meacham died in 1796 after nine years of leadership. Following his death, Lucy Wright assumed full duties of the lead ministry. She was 36 years of age and would hold the office until her death 25 years later. After her death, leadership was provided by a group of leaders in Mount Lebanon ("the central ministry"), with no individual again having as much authority as she had. Wright's selection met some resistance at first, but Meacham's confidence in her was not misplaced, and she proved to be a very effective and aggressive Shaker leader. She reopened "the testimony," personally selecting individuals to undertake missionary duties. She established a "gathering order" as a means to bring into the villages individuals who were prospects for membership but who needed more teaching and preparation before acceptance into the society.

Having heard about the religious revivals taking place in the West, Lucy Wright sent missionaries to make the long trek to Kentucky. This was without doubt the most important decision of her tenure and would result in the establishment of Shaker villages in Kentucky, Ohio, and Indiana.

ANN LEE TOMBSTONE. The tombstone lists February 29, 1736, as her date of birth, although it is uncertain. The grave of Lucy Wright is adjacent. The cemetery was originally in a different location but was relocated due to an expansion of the nearby Albany International Airport. The cemetery is part of the Watervliet Shaker site, operated by the Shaker Heritage Society. (Courtesy of Shaker Heritage Society.)

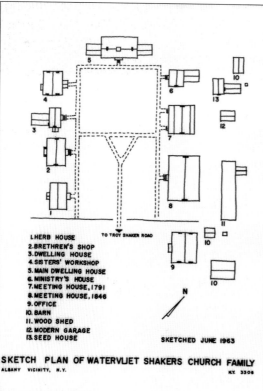

1. HERB HOUSE
2. BRETHREN'S SHOP
3. DWELLING HOUSE
4. SISTERS' WORKSHOP
5. MAIN DWELLING HOUSE
6. MINISTRY'S HOUSE
7. MEETING HOUSE, 1791
8. MEETING HOUSE, 1846
9. OFFICE
10. BARN
11. WOOD SHED
12. MODERN GARAGE
13. SEED HOUSE

TO TROY SHAKER ROAD

N

SKETCHED JUNE 1963

SKETCH PLAN OF WATERVLIET SHAKERS CHURCH FAMILY
ALBANY VICINITY, N.Y.   NY 3305

WATERVLIET CHURCH FAMILY. The photograph, taken during the 1920s, shows the Watervliet Church Family "inner yard," looking north. The annotated sketch identifies the various buildings. All of the buildings except the 1791 Meeting House were built after 1800. The Church Family had other buildings not shown in the picture, including a schoolhouse, mill, and washhouse/canning factory. (Courtesy of Library of Congress, Prints and Photographs Division, HABS.)

EARLY SHAKER MEETINGHOUSES. The second Watervliet Meeting House (on the left) was built in 1791, replacing a log structure built in 1784. It was designed by Moses Johnson of Enfield, New Hampshire, who designed and oversaw construction of 10 similar gambrel-roofed Shaker meetinghouses between 1785 and 1794, the first of which was at New Lebanon. This photograph was made during the 1920s, and the building was demolished in 1927. The replacement Meeting House (on the right) was built in 1846 and still stands. (Courtesy of Library of Congress, Prints and Photographs Division, HABS.)

NEW LEBANON CHURCH FAMILY. This photograph provides a perspective view of some Church Family buildings, including the arch-roofed Meeting House in the center. Clusters of buildings of the other families remain, some occupied by the Darrow School, named for the Shaker converts who provided the land to the society. The Shaker Museum and Library has undertaken restoration of 10 North Family buildings as the new home for the museum, including the "great stone barn"—the largest stone barn in America. The location was referred to as Mount Lebanon beginning in the 1860s. (Courtesy of Library of Congress, Prints and Photographs Division, HABS.) .

Three

THE SECOND GREAT AWAKENING

Kentucky achieved statehood in 1792, having previously been part of Virginia. Soon thereafter, in 1798, a sequence of revivals began in southern Kentucky, culminating with the best known of the revivals at Cane Ridge in 1801. Collectively these revivals are referred to as the Second Great Awakening, or the Kentucky Revival.

The so-called Great Awakening of the 1730s and 1740s occurred in the New England and middle colonies, with similar revival activities underway in England, Scotland, and Northern Ireland. The preaching of Congregationalist Jonathan Edwards in New England is considered to mark the beginning of the Great Awakening in America. Church of England minister George Whitefield preached at revival services on both sides of the Atlantic, including audiences as large as 30,000 in Scotland during 1742. Huge numbers were reported to be converted, with various "physical exercises," including swooning.

Economic conditions after the Revolutionary War led to a migration across the mountains to Tennessee and Kentucky. The first of the Kentucky revivals occurred in Logan County, resulting from the preaching of James McGready, who moved to the county in 1796 as minister for three small Presbyterian congregations named for rivers: Red, Muddy, and Gasper. McGready and his "boys" (Conkin 1990) answered the call for ministers in the Cumberland region along the Tennessee-Kentucky border. McGready and William McGee came first, soon followed by John Rankin, William Hodge, and William McAdow. McGready had previously served a church in Guilford County, North Carolina, and had preached frequently at David Caldwell's nearby academy, leading to many conversions and a revival among the students.

McGready began revival preparations as soon as he arrived, leading to the beginning of a great revival in 1798. First at Gasper River, and then at Muddy River and Red River, revival excitement and conversions occurred beginning with the young people. The next year's summer communion services resulted in a continuation of the revival, with "extreme physical exercises" (groaning, swooning, crying). By the summer of 1800, word had spread widely about the earlier revivals, and in June, communion was held in the small log Red River Meeting House, with dozens falling down in their religious fervor. The second communion of the summer was held in July at Gasper River, with people coming from great distances. One notable aspect of the Gasper River revival was that a great many families arrived with provisions to camp on the grounds, marking the beginning of the camp meeting trend in America. Some likely had camped at Red River the previous month. The revival at Muddy River was also very well attended.

By 1800, the fertile farmland of the bluegrass area was attracting many settlers. Word of the great revivals in the southern part of the state brought about interest, and during the winter of 1800–1801, religious activity increased throughout central Kentucky. Baptists, Methodists, and Presbyterians all reported successes. During 1801, revivals were beginning to occur all over the country, including New England, the mid-Atlantic region, the South, and the newly settled West.

Barton W. Stone began his first full-time work in 1798 as the minister for the Presbyterian churches at Cane Ridge and Concord in Bourbon County. He was educated at the academy of David Caldwell in Virginia, where he heard the revival preaching of McGready and was moved to greater spiritual commitment by the preaching of young William Hodge. In early May 1801, he visited his former associates McGready and Rankin at Gasper River and observed and participated in a communion service there. Much later he wrote about it (Stone 1847):

> My conviction was complete that it was a good work—the work of God; nor has my mind wavered since on the subject. Much did I then see, and much have I since seen, that I considered to be fanaticism; but this should not condemn the work.

He returned home and reported these events to his congregations, which resulted in the occurrence of similar physical exercises. In late May, the five-day communion service was held at Concord, with neighboring Presbyterians and Methodists participating, again with similar results. Other notable revivals were held in the spring and summer of 1801, including one at Cabin Creek in late May, where Richard McNemar, a former Cane Ridge elder, was the minister.

On Friday, August 6, 1801, people started arriving at Cane Ridge for the annual communion. The local congregation had erected a tent for outdoor preaching, as was the custom of the time. People kept arriving for days, all with great anticipation. Huge numbers of people camped on the grounds, estimated to include 140 wagons and carriages for the weekend events. People brought food to prepare in the open and corn or hay for their horses. Barton Stone was host minister, with Matthew Houston presenting the first sermon on Friday evening. On Saturday, the crowds continued to grow. Estimates of the crowd size vary greatly, but it is likely that 20,000 or more were there for one or more days. John Lyle preached in the tent, followed by "the wild young Richard McNemar, who preached like a Methodist, with ecstasy and joy reflected on his face" (Conkin 1990). Due to the crowds and level of response, unscheduled evening sermons were presented by Lyle, McNemar, and Houston. A contemporary report of the noise on the grounds described it as like the roar of Niagara.

The communion—the primary reason for the gathering—took place on Sunday. Robert Marshall, minister of a nearby congregation, preached outside at the tent, and then those having been granted communion tokens moved inside the meetinghouse to participate. The best estimate is that about 900 took communion, no doubt entering "in shifts." Only Presbyterian ministers presided at the communion, although several Methodist ministers preached, and some Baptists preached on the grounds. Numerous lay people exhorted on the grounds, including new converts. Prominent Methodist minister William Burke arranged a make-shift pulpit about 15 feet high on a partially fallen tree about 100 feet east of the meetinghouse, where he had a large response. Reportedly there were four primary centers of activity: the tent, the meetinghouse, Burke's "pulpit," and an assembly of black people.

People from all walks of life came to Cane Ridge, including Kentucky governor James Garrard, members of the local gentry, farmers, laborers, and slaves. The communion was reportedly orderly and solemn, with some weeping at the tables. But the grounds were quite different. There was groaning and falling, some with weak knees and a light head. Some who fell were in a trance, some with an apparent seizure, while others spoke and were responsive. Perhaps 1,000 fell to the ground "slain." Those assembled gradually left the grounds, while others kept coming until at least Wednesday, with many reluctant to leave.

This revival stands as one of the most written about and most famous in American history. The momentum that spurred the Cane Ridge revival was further energized by the amazing events that occurred there. And while attention would turn to revivals in other locations, the role to be played by Cane Ridge in America's religious history was by no means yet completed.

RED RIVER MEETING HOUSE. These images show the rebuilt log Red River Meeting House in Logan County, Kentucky, and a marker summarizing the site's history. A large cemetery is adjacent. Some attendees camped on the grounds here during the great revival of June 1800, but the Gasper River church is considered to be the location of the first "intentional" camp meeting in July 1800. (Photographs by the author.)

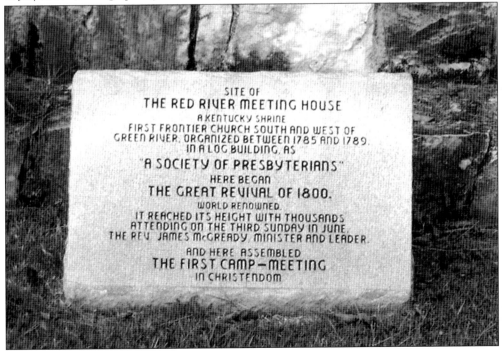

SITE OF
THE RED RIVER MEETING HOUSE
A KENTUCKY SHRINE
FIRST FRONTIER CHURCH SOUTH AND WEST OF
GREEN RIVER, ORGANIZED BETWEEN 1785 AND 1789,
IN A LOG BUILDING, AS
"A SOCIETY OF PRESBYTERIANS"
HERE BEGAN
THE GREAT REVIVAL OF 1800,
WORLD RENOWNED.
IT REACHED ITS HEIGHT WITH THOUSANDS
ATTENDING ON THE THIRD SUNDAY IN JUNE,
THE REV. JAMES McGREADY, MINISTER AND LEADER.
AND HERE ASSEMBLED
THE FIRST CAMP—MEETING
IN CHRISTENDOM

CANE RIDGE MEETING HOUSE. Built in 1791, the Meeting House is located eight miles east of Paris, Kentucky. Considered to be among the largest one-room log buildings in America, it measures 30 by 50 feet. The walls are built of blue ash logs, and the beams and roof supports are of oak and chestnut. Built for use by a Presbyterian congregation, it was the site of the great revival of 1801, with many thousands gathered on the grounds. It is the birthplace of the Christian/New Light movement and was used by the Cane Ridge Christian Church until 1921. (Courtesy of the Cane Ridge Preservation Project.)

CANE RIDGE TODAY. During the 1950s, the old Meeting House was enclosed by a protective building constructed of limestone. Barton W. Stone and many early settlers are buried in the adjacent cemetery. A museum emphasizing the history of Cane Ridge and the Stone/Campbell movement is housed in a separate building. (Courtesy of the Cane Ridge Preservation Project; cemetery photograph by the author.)

BARTON W. STONE. Barton Warren Stone was the minister at Cane Ridge during the great revival. Along with Richard McNemar and other fellow Presbyterian ministers, he became disillusioned with Presbyterian doctrine and was a leader in the Christian or New Light movement. The Disciples of Christ, independent Christian churches, and Churches of Christ all credit Stone with a significant role in their histories. (Courtesy of the Cane Ridge Preservation Project.)

GOV. JAMES GARRARD. Garrard served as the second governor of Kentucky (1796–1804). A resident of Bourbon County, he attended the Cane Ridge revival and experienced "physical manifestations." A former Baptist minister, he was considered to be an apostate unitarian at the time. Born in Virginia in 1749, he served in the Revolutionary War and died in 1822. Garrard County, Kentucky, is named for him. (Courtesy of Kentucky Historical Society.)

THE

KENTUCKY REVIVAL,

OR,

A SHORT HISTORY

OF THE LATE EXTRAORDINARY OUT-POURING OF THE
SPIRIT OF GOD, IN THE WESTERN STATES OF
AMERICA, AGREEABLY TO SCRIPTURE-
PROMISES, AND PROPHECIES CON-
CERNING THE LATTER DAY:

WITH A BRIEF ACCOUNT

OF THE ENTRANCE AND PROGRESS OF WHAT
THE WORLD CALL

SHAKERISM,

AMONG THE SUBJECTS OF THE LATE REVIVAL
IN *OHIO* AND *KENTUCKY.*

PRESENTED TO THE
TRUE ZION-TRAVELLER,
AS A MEMORIAL OF THE WILDERNESS JOURNEY.

BY RICHARD M'NEMAR.

" When ye see a cloud rise out of the west, straightway ye say,
" there cometh a shower ; and so it is : And when YE FEEL
" the south wind blow, ye say, there will be heat ; and it
" cometh to pass—Can ye not discern the signs of the times."

CHRIST.

1808.

COLLEGE PRESS, Joplin, Missouri

McNEMAR'S *The Kentucky Revival.* Richard McNemar was first a Presbyterian minister, then briefly a Christian/New Light minister, and became a Shaker in 1805. By 1808, when he published *The Kentucky Revival,* he was on his way to becoming known as one of the most talented and influential Shakers in the new western societies. Reviewing the history of the great revival, his goal was to present Shaker doctrine to those who had participated in the revival, among whom a "very extraordinary and singular work of God . . . has been wrought" but who had "pitched their tents short of mount Zion." (Courtesy of Dr. Hans Rollman, Memorial University of Newfoundland.)

Four

SHAKER CONVERTS IN KENTUCKY

Richard McNemar began to teach "free will" as opposed to divine election and that the millennium was at hand, and he encouraged unrestrained physical exercises in worship. This led to charges being brought against him to the presbytery. He soon moved from Cabin Creek to a church at Turtle Creek northeast of Cincinnati. Allied with him were his brother-in-law John Dunlavy and John Thompson, minister for the Springfield church near Cincinnati. Barton Stone also had growing doubts about some aspects of Calvinism and was a strong advocate for Christian unity.

In 1803, the new Kentucky Synod, meeting in Lexington, heard charges against McNemar and Thompson. Stone, Dunlavy, and Robert Marshall (minister of a church near Lexington) supported McNemar and Thompson. According to Stone (1847), "In a short recess of the Synod, we five withdrew to a private garden, where, after prayer for direction . . . with a perfect unanimity drew up a protest against the proceedings of the Synod in McNemar's case, and a declaration of our independence, and of our withdrawal from their jurisdiction, but not from their communion." They claimed the right to interpret scriptures for themselves. The five men constituted themselves into the "Springfield Presbytery" (named for Thompson's church) (McNemar 1808).

The new presbytery accepted into the ministry without formal ordination Malcolm Worley, an associate of McNemar, and David Purviance, an associate of Stone. After less than a year, they decided to disband the Springfield Presbytery, generating a document entitled "The Last Will and Testament of the Springfield Presbytery," written by McNemar. Stone wrote, "With the man-made creeds we threw it overboard, and took the name *Christian*—the name given to disciples by divine appointment first at Antioch" (Stone 1847). The movement was also referred to as "new lights" and "schismatics." From the movement were eventually to result three "restoration" churches—Disciples of Christ (following the 1832 merger with churches influenced by Alexander Campbell), independent Christian churches, and Churches of Christ. Continuing issues within the Presbyterian Church resulted in formation of the Cumberland Presbyterian Church in 1810.

Having dissolved their presbytery, and their followers making up independent local churches, McNemar, Stone, and their colleagues continued their quest for biblical truth. They were thus separated from established doctrine, searching for truth, and in a state of high expectation. The Shakers would soon benefit. Along with most of the country, Lucy Wright learned of the revival activities in the West and saw it as a possible fulfillment of what Ann Lee had earlier predicted: "The next opening of the gospel will be in the south-west; it will be at a great distance; and there will be a great work of God," and "You may live to see it, but I shall not."

Wright selected three individuals well suited to this missionary effort: Elder Benjamin Seth Youngs, Issachar Bates, and John Meacham, eldest son of Joseph Meacham. They loaded their baggage on a horse and departed from New Lebanon on January 1, 1805, bound for Lexington, Kentucky, walking most of the way—over 1,000 miles. They traveled through the Cumberland Gap into Kentucky. Learning about a Christian church at Paint Lick, they attended worship on Sunday, March 3, and had private discussions with the minister, Matthew Houston. On March

7, Youngs was permitted to speak before 150 people, reading a letter of introduction from the New Lebanon ministry.

Houston suggested that the missionaries visit Cane Ridge, where, as Bates later wrote, "they sucked in our light as greedily as ever an ox drank water" (Ham 1962). Barton Stone was initially favorably impressed with the missionaries but soon became a staunch opponent. On March 29, the missionaries visited with Malcolm Worley at his home in Ohio, and five days later, he became the first Shaker convert in the West. McNemar confessed his sins on April 24 and would become a major force for the Shaker cause. Ham (1962) observed that without McNemar's support, "the Shaker mission might well have ended in failure," and that he "stands out as the most able and gifted of the believers in the West." McNemar was married with seven children, but like all the Shaker believers, he now committed to a life of celibacy. Within a month, over 30 members of McNemar's churches had converted. At Beulah, John Houston became the first Shaker convert in October 1805, and by 1808, there were 55 believers. In July 1805, John Dunlavy became a believer, and 66 were converted from his congregations (Eagle Creek and Strait Creek). Nearby in Kentucky, 18 were converted at Limestone, Cabin Creek, and Washington. The numerous conversions, and an appeal from the missionaries, led the New Lebanon ministry to send David Darrow to become the primary leader in the West. He arrived at Turtle Creek, Ohio, in July 1805.

Barton Stone had earlier invited the Shakers to the August 1805 communion at Concord. McNemar, Dunlavy, Worley, and Youngs attended. By that time, Stone was firmly opposed to Shaker teaching, rejecting their beliefs about the millennium and celibacy, among others. Given the confidence the Bourbon County churches had in Stone, the Shakers made no headway with his "flock." But attending that day were three members of a Christian group in Mercer County, Kentucky: Elisha Thomas and brothers Samuel and Henry Banta. They met privately with Youngs and accepted the Shaker faith. A major success for the Shakers occurred in the conversion of Matthew Houston in February 1806. "His tact and his knowledge of revival phenomena made him western Shakerism's master psychologist in dealing with converts and young Believers" (Ham 1962). In the spring of 1806, several Shaker families settled on the 140-acre Shawnee Run farm of Elisha Thomas, the beginnings of what was to become the Pleasant Hill society.

By September 1806, it was apparent that Stone, Marshall, and Thompson had thwarted Shaker efforts among the Cane Ridge, Concord, Bethel, and Springfield Christian fellowships. Youngs and Bates " 'shook the dust . . . of wicked Cane Ridge' from their feet" (Ham 1962). In September 1807, Bates, McNemar, and Houston traveled to the "Cumberland Country." The Gasper River church was at that time experiencing a struggle between the Cumberland Presbytery and the Synod of Kentucky regarding licensing of ministers and free will versus divine election. John Rankin, local minister and a leader in the Cumberland Presbytery, was converted. Bates returned in January 1808 to increase the number of believers to 50 and also converted 20 at Red Banks. The Gasper River believers would become the nucleus of the South Union village.

In April 1808, Bates, Dunlavy, Houston, and James Hodge visited the Shaker converts at Shawnee Run, Gasper River, and Red Banks, and then traveled to Knox County, Indiana, where a Christian group worshiped on Busseron Creek. The missionaries spent six weeks there, preaching to crowds of over 400. They converted over 70, including three Christian preachers, resulting in the Busro Shaker settlement. This would be the last major effort to benefit from the effects of the Second Great Awakening.

By 1810, Darrow reported 1,280 "young believers" in the West, which equaled the number of Shakers in the East. Lucy Wright's missionary initiative in the West, begun five years earlier, had resulted in societies in Kentucky (Pleasant Hill and South Union), Ohio (North Union, Union Village, Watervliet, and later Whitewater), and Indiana (West Union). Darrow now turned his attention to establishing gospel order among the Western believers.

PRIMITIVE HOUSES AT PLEASANT HILL AND SOUTH UNION. In the early days of Shaker ingathering at Shawnee Run and Gasper (later Pleasant Hill and South Union, respectively), they used the existing homes of converts until suitable communal dwellings could be built. At South Union, the Shakers also built log structures in the early days, using many of them throughout the 19th century. These images show homes at Pleasant Hill (above) and South Union still in use at a later time. They are likely somewhat representative of the original dwellings on property that became part of society land holdings. (Courtesy of the Shaker Village of Pleasant Hill [above] and Canterbury Shaker Village [below].)

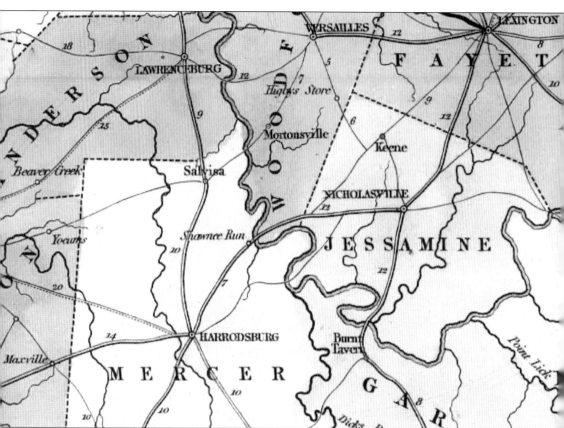

SEGMENTS OF 1839 KENTUCKY MAP. On this and the following page are segments from the "Map of Kentucky & Tennessee exhibiting the post offices, post roads, canals, rail roads, &c.; by David. H. Burr (Late topographer to the Post Office,) Geographer to the House of Representatives of the U.S. . . . From his *The American Atlas* (London, J. Arrowsmith, 1839)." The map segment

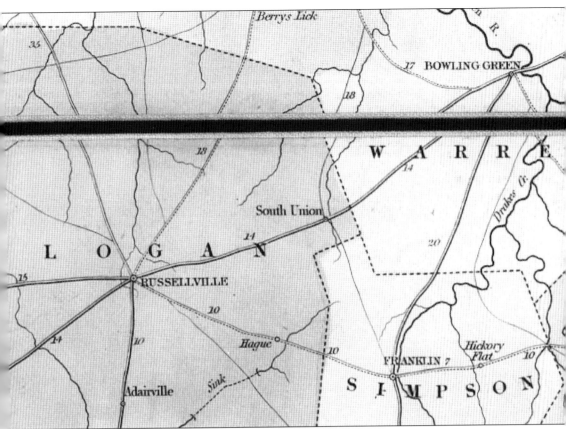

above left shows Pleasant Hill as "Shawnee Run," its prior designation. It is seen on later maps as either Shakertown or Pleasant Hill. The segment above right shows South Union. The separator between the northwest and southwest quadrants of the map crosses this segment. (Courtesy of Library of Congress, Geography and Map Division, http://memory.loc.gov/ammem/gmdhtml/.)

A BRIEF

HISTORICAL ACCOUNT

OF SUNDRY THINGS IN THE DOCTRINES AND STATE OF

THE CHRISTIAN, OR AS IT IS COMMONLY CALLED,

THE NEWLIGHT CHURCH.

BY R. MARSHAL & J THOMPSON,
Ministers of the Gospel, and Members of said Church.

CONTAINING THEIR TESTIMONY AGAINST SEVERAL DOC-
TRINES HELD IN THAT CHURCH, AND ITS DISORGANI-
ZED STATE; TOGETHER WITH SOME REASONS WHY
THOSE TWO BRETHREN PURPOSE TO SEEK FOR A MORE
PURE AND ORDERLY CONNEXION.

Prove all things ; hold fast that which is good—PAUL.

CINCINNATI:
PUBLISHED BY J. CARPENTER & Co.
CORNER OF MAIN & FIFTH STREETS.

1811.

A Brief Historical Account BY MARSHALL AND THOMPSON. The Presbyterian ministers who led the breakaway Christian/New Light movement were Richard McNemar, Barton Stone, John Thompson, John Dunlavy, and Robert Marshall. They formed the Springfield Presbytery (which they later dissolved) and accepted into ministry Malcolm Worley and David Purviance. Of these seven, McNemar, Dunlavy, and Worley subsequently became Shakers, while Marshall and Thompson returned to the Presbyterian Church. This image shows the title page of a document by Marshall and Thompson explaining their action. (Courtesy of Dr. Hans Rollman, Memorial University of Newfoundland.)

Five

VILLAGES AND FARMS

Development of all the Shaker villages—East and West—followed much the same pattern: new converts who were landowners would turn over their land and homes to the society, and a communal village would gradually be developed. David Darrow was one of the first converts at New Lebanon, and his former farm had become the site of the New Lebanon Shaker village. After relocating to the West, "Father David" oversaw the development of the communal village at Turtle Creek and, from that location, directed the spiritual and temporal activities of all the believers in the West.

The first permanent communal gathering of believers in Kentucky occurred on Shawnee Run in Mercer County in the spring of 1806, on the 140-acre farm of Elisha Thomas. In December of that year, 44 adult converts signed a covenant, "dedicating themselves and their property to the material benefit of each other." In January 1809, John Meacham, Samuel Turner, Lucy Smith, and Anna Cole were appointed elders, with Meacham as first or lead elder. In November 1809, Comstock Betts, Joseph Allen, Molly Goodrich, and Mercy Pickett were appointed elders at Gasper in Logan County. Due to lack of satisfaction with Betts in the role, Darrow replaced him with Benjamin Seth Youngs as lead elder in October 1811. All of the original elders at Shawnee Run and Gasper were Eastern Shakers experienced in the faith. Trustees were soon appointed to conduct business with the world. In 1811, the Shawnee Run society was renamed Pleasant Hill, and in 1813, Gasper became South Union (named for Union Village, the new name for the Turtle Creek society).

Adding to the 140-acre Elisha Thomas farm, in 1807, Samuel Banta provided 302 acres on which the Pleasant Hill village would be built. At Gasper, convert Jesse McComb provided his 250 acres and home to the society. The villages organized according to the arrangement Joseph Meacham had directed at New Lebanon, which had already been implemented in the Western oversight village of Turtle Creek. Each society planned a village that reflected the organization, with a meetinghouse in the center of the new village and a "center family" dwelling across the street. The center family was made up of committed believers who were considered able to serve as examples of faithfulness and service to the other families. The family was the operational unit of the Shaker organization, with the goal for each to be self-sufficient, and typically numbering from 50 to 100 members. Each family had its own dwelling house, washhouse, farmland, barns, and shops and carried out its own small industries. Reflecting the structure of the full Shaker society, in time, each family would have its own elders and eldresses and deacons and deaconesses. South Union eventually had four families, and Pleasant Hill had five. The families came to the aid of others as needed, to help out with unusual work demands or when some disaster struck. The villages cooperated among themselves in similar ways.

Since the livelihood of the Kentucky Shakers was expected to come to a great extent from agriculture, both societies were aggressive in expanding their land holdings. South Union eventually had about 6,000 acres of land, and Pleasant Hill holdings reached about 4,400 acres.

Adjacent land was frequently purchased by means of a down payment and three additional annual payments. The farmland of both societies was excellent, fertile, and mostly tillable, though some was "new ground" and had to be "grubbed" when purchased. Both societies had wooded tracts—South Union less so—which were important to their building programs, along with good water sources and good transportation routes. Pleasant Hill was near the Kentucky River, on which they purchased a ferry landing site, and South Union was not far from the Red River, so both societies had access to water routes. The villages were situated along good (for the time) roads, providing good access to towns and markets. Pleasant Hill was near Harrodsburg, and South Union was between Russellville and Bowling Green.

The name of Micajah Burnett is widely known relative to the development of Pleasant Hill, and he was of assistance at South Union and Union Village as well. His January 10, 1879, obituary, from Pleasant Hill's *Church Record Book A*, indicated that he was 87 as of the previous May 13, that he "was among the worthiest, having spent his life from early youth in this sacred cause," and that "he was the principal Architect of this Village—an accomplished Civil Engineer, a Masterly Mathemetician, a competent Surveyor, a Mechanic & Machinist of the first order, a good Mill Wright and withal a firmly established honest hearted Christian Shaker beloved, respected & honored by all." In the 1850 U.S. census, his occupation was given as architect, in 1860 as carpenter, and in 1870 as engineer. His achievements are especially noteworthy considering that he apparently had little or no formal training. He is often credited with devising the layout of the village and designing most of the buildings, but the full extent of his contributions is uncertain from the written records.

The buildings whose construction Burnett oversaw are functional, beautiful, and have well withstood the ravages of time. The East Family house took three years to complete, involving quarrying stone from the Kentucky River Gorge, digging clay to make bricks, cutting timber, sawing and hewing beams, and planing finish lumber. He oversaw the work of many helpers, next completing the West Family House in 1822. He then undertook construction of the Centre House, to replace a previous dwelling. Due to various delays, this building was not completed until 1834. The Pleasant Hill Centre House and Meeting House are considered by many to be the most outstanding in the village. Numerous Shaker meetinghouses in the East were designed by Moses Johnson between 1785 and 1794, all with similar gambrel-roof designs. A truss-roof construction was used for the Meeting House at Pleasant Hill, leaving the interior fully open to accommodate the worship activities. The heavy limestone foundation and exceptionally strong walls were designed to accommodate the expected vibration from the dancing during worship. The building designs reflect both the guidance from New Lebanon and influence of the Federal style then popular. A particularly well-known design usually attributed to Micajah Burnett is the beautiful twin spiral staircases in the Trustees' Office. He also oversaw development of the water system at Pleasant Hill and those at South Union and Union Village (Ohio).

At South Union, a very active building program was also undertaken. In 1813, they undertook to replace the small existing meetinghouse, completing a two-story structure in 1818, with foundation of stone they cut and of brick made at the village. The present Centre House was begun in 1822 and completed in 1833. The four-story interior includes beautiful arches and open functional spaces. Two sets of stairways were provided, one for the sisters and one for the brethren. They spent a great deal of time and effort on their operational structures, building sawmills, gristmill, fulling mill, mill dam, shops, and barns.

By the early 1820s, there were approximately 490 believers at Pleasant Hill and 350 at South Union (Nordhoff 1875). They had accomplished a very great deal in a short length of time and were now well-housed, had large farms made up of some of the best land in Kentucky, and were situated to provide most of their needed support functions and to bring in income by selling products and services to their neighbors. Their prosperity and achievements in contrast with their neighbors was striking, testifying to commitment, hard work, and effective leadership.

PLEASANT HILL PERSPECTIVE. This contemporary photograph shows Pleasant Hill's beautiful rolling setting. The Tanyard Brick Shop is in the foreground, with the main part of the village in the distance. No doubt it was considered important to have the tanyard odors at a good distance from dwellings and shops. (Courtesy of the Shaker Village of Pleasant Hill.)

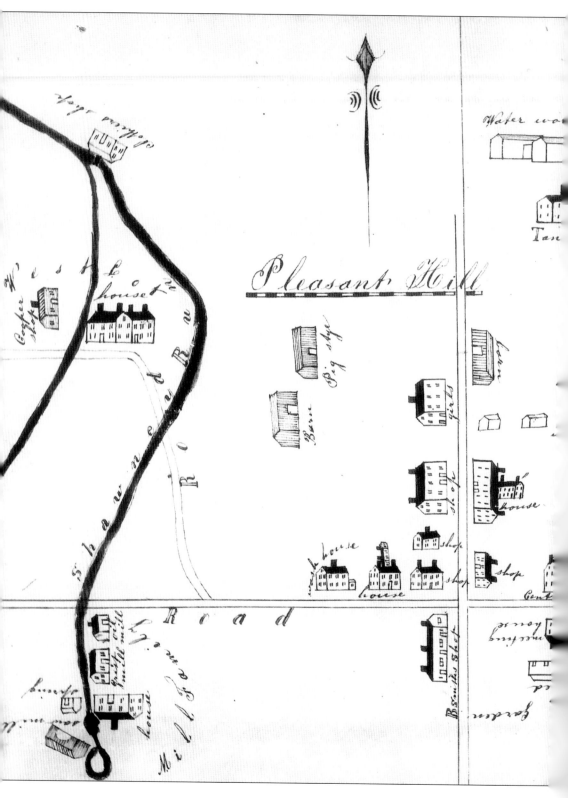

Pleasant Hill

Office shop

Coopers shop

First house

Shawneed Road

Pig sty

Barn

girls

house

Water wo...

Tan

house

shop

house

wash house

house

shop

shop

shop

Cent...

Road

B smiths Shop

Mill Road

grist mill

house

B smith

Garden

...ning house

40

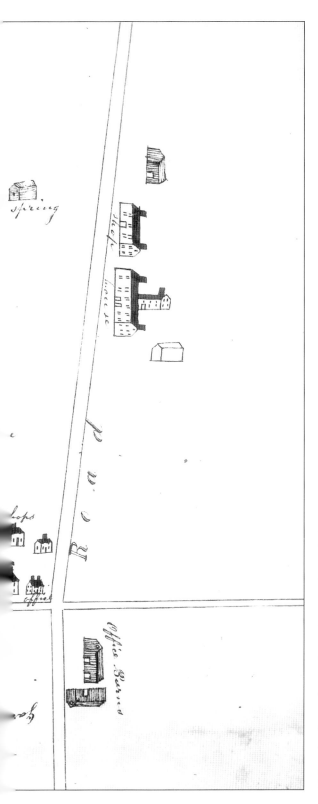

HAND-DRAWN MAP OF PLEASANT HILL, 1835. This sketch is from an 11-page document with the cover page reading: "Sketches of the various Societies of Belivers [i.e. Believers] in the states of Ohio & Kentucky. To which is added a slight sketch of Sodus Bay in the northern part of N. York. Also a map containing several of the states on which is laid out the route of Br. Rufus Bishop and Isaac N. Youngs New Lebanon while on a tour to visit these societies, in the summer and fall of 1834. Copied from Isaac N. Youngs' Journal, July 1835 by George Kendall." (Courtesy of Library of Congress, Geography and Map Division, Cultural Landscapes collection.)

MICAJAH BURNETT. This sketch of the talented designer and builder was made by a contemporary, Constantine Rafinesque, professor at Transylvania University. Born in 1791, Burnett came to Pleasant Hill with his parents at age 17. With little or no formal training, he oversaw development of many outstanding buildings at Pleasant Hill and helped with projects at South Union, also. He died in 1879. (Courtesy of C. S. Rafinesque Collection, Special Collections and Archives, Transylvania University, Lexington, Kentucky. Permission granted for one-time use only.)

PLEASANT HILL 1809 CENTRE HOUSE. This was among the first permanent buildings at Pleasant Hill. Constructed of limestone, it is two and one-half stories tall, with a partial basement. The small structure on the right is the cellar entrance. The building does not exhibit as many beautiful features as later ones, but the storage unit underneath a stairway reflects the consistent attention to detail. A replacement Centre House was completed in 1815, and from it the Centre Family moved to the 1834 Centre House. This building later served as the Farm Deacon's Shop. The 1815 Centre House was later destroyed by fire. (Courtesy of Library of Congress, Prints and Photographs Division, HABS.)

PLEASANT HILL 1820 MEETING HOUSE. The Meeting House is considered by many to be one of the two finest Pleasant Hill buildings—the other being the existing Centre Dwelling House. Very different from the Eastern meetinghouses designed by Moses Johnson, it has a truss-roof construction and is built on a heavy limestone foundation with exceptionally strong walls to accommodate the vibration from dancing. Its dimensions are 60 by 44 feet. Brothers and sisters entered through separate doors (left and right, respectively) and sat on separate sides. The ministry occupied the second-floor rooms and observed Sunday worship services from small windows in the stairways. (Courtesy of Library of Congress, Prints and Photographs Division, HABS.)

PLEASANT HILL 1822 WEST FAMILY HOUSE. This is another of the numerous buildings whose construction was overseen by Micajah Burnett. This is a view of the side and rear of the building. The East Family House had been completed in 1819 and was similar in appearance to this one, but it had three floors. Burnett next undertook building the massive new Centre House. (Courtesy of Library of Congress, Prints and Photographs Division, HABS.)

PLEASANT HILL 1834 CENTRE HOUSE. This building is the crowning achievement of the building program at Pleasant Hill and is among the most impressive buildings in all the Shaker villages. It served as the home for as many as 80 Shakers of the Centre Family. The stone structure was made of limestone from the nearby Kentucky River palisades, quarried by the Shakers, and consists of 24,960 square feet in 40 rooms. (Courtesy of Library of Congress, Prints and Photographs Division, HABS.)

PLEASANT HILL 1834 CENTRE HOUSE INTERIOR. The functionality, beauty, and workmanship of this building can be seen in some interior details. The scene above shows the first-floor hallway, looking toward the back of the dual stairways to the second floor and the stairway doors to the cellar below. Note the pegs on the walls, used in this case to hang chairs. The view below is of the second-floor hallway, with separate stairways for the brethren and sisters. Other views within this building are included in later chapters. (Courtesy of Library of Congress, Prints and Photographs Division, HABS.)

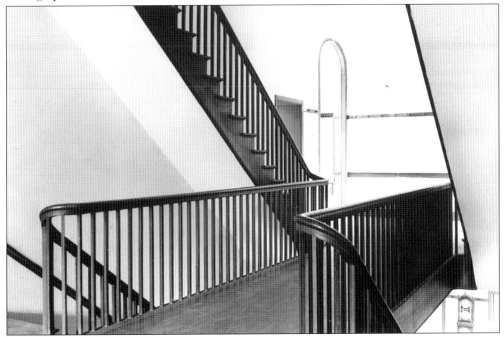

PLEASANT HILL TRUSTEES' OFFICE. This building was completed in 1841, designed by Micajah Burnett. The trustees were the financial managers of the society, and this building served as their office and the place where they conducted business with the world. It also provided overnight lodging to visiting Shakers and people from the world. The photographs show the front (above) and left side and rear (below) of the building. Note the arched doors in the side of the building. (Courtesy of Library of Congress, Prints and Photographs Division, HABS.)

PLEASANT HILL TRUSTEES' OFFICE STAIRWAYS. The graceful twin spiral stairways in the Trustees' Office are admired as a Micajah Burnett masterpiece. The three-story stairways are anchored at the top and bottom and at each of the intermediate floors. The bent cherry handrails are a notable feature, especially given the relatively primitive tools and methods of the time. (Courtesy of Library of Congress, Prints and Photographs Division, HABS.)

PLEASANT HILL 1834 WATER SYSTEM. The water system was developed under Micajah Burnett's oversight. The system operated from the Water House (at the left in the photograph). A large cypress cistern, elevated on stone piers, was filled from a spring one-half mile downhill by means of horses on a treadmill pump. Water was distributed by gravity flow to kitchens, bathhouses, and washhouses through lead pipes. The Centre Family Brethren's Bath House is the smaller building in the photograph. It is thought to be the first such water supply system in Kentucky. (Courtesy of Library of Congress, Prints and Photographs Division, HABS.)

AERIAL VIEW OF SOUTH UNION. This striking scene provides an indication of the excellent farmland at South Union. The Centre House is at the lower right, with the Wash House to the left, and the Smoke and Milk House to the right of the Wash House. The long mound along the right side of the Wash House is the Mound Cistern. The small building near the front of the barn is the Steam House. A letter from Pleasant Hill to Lucy Wright in 1807 described South Union (Gasper River) as "almost an hundred and thirty miles from here" and "as level and beautiful habitation as almost any to be found in the world" (Neal 1982). (Courtesy of Shaker Museum at South Union.)

SOUTH UNION 1810 BUILDING. This was one of the first permanent buildings constructed at South Union and the longest-surviving of all the Centre Family frame buildings, standing for more than a century. Located on the north side of the main street, west of the Centre House, it served as the schoolhouse for the society's children after earlier serving as a dwelling. The 1922 photograph below shows its location relative to the Centre House. There were 100 children at South Union in 1812 (Neal 1947). A journal entry for December 23, 1844, states: "School commenced to day . . . 19 schollars teacher J. Rankin." (Courtesy of Western Reserve Historical Society [above] and Shaker Museum at South Union [below].)

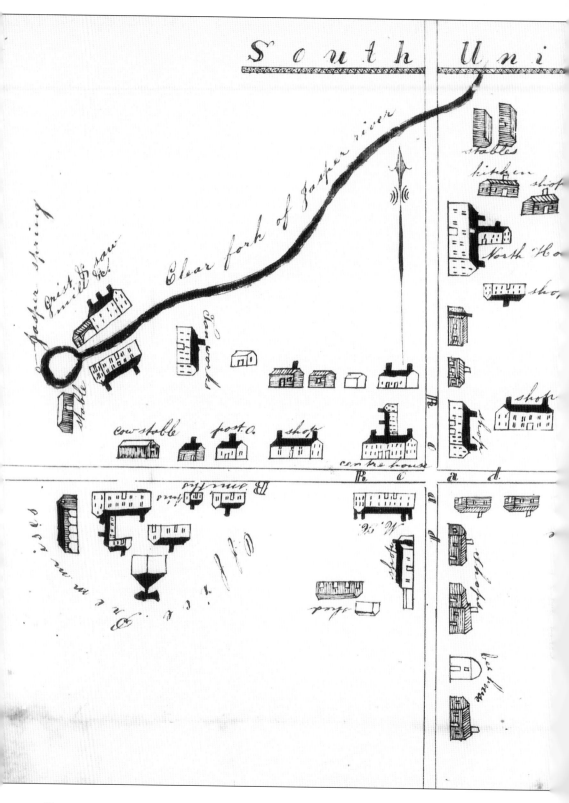

South Uni

stables

kitchen

shop

North Ho

shop

shop

shop

Jasper Spring

grist & saw mill &c.

Clear fork of Jasper river

Tan works

stable

cow stable

post O.

shop

centre house

Road

Road

Brewery

Brewery shed

W. H.

shop

shed

shops

hen house

52

HAND-DRAWN MAP OF SOUTH UNION, 1835. Like the map of Pleasant Hill on pages 40 and 41, this sketch is from an 11-page document with cover page reading, "Sketches of the various Societies of Belivers [i.e. Believers] in the states of Ohio & Kentucky. To which is added a slight sketch of Sodus Bay in the northern part of N. York. Also a map containing several of the states on which is laid out the route of Br. Rufus Bishop and Isaac N. Youngs New Lebanon while on a tour to visit these societies, in the summer and fall of 1834. Copied from Isaac N. Youngs' Journal, July 1835 by George Kendall." (Courtesy of Library of Congress, Geography & Map Division, Cultural Landscapes collection.)

SOUTH UNION 1815 CENTRE HOUSE. This was the first brick building constructed at South Union. The bricks were made by the brethren in their own brick kilns. The photograph below shows a portion of the newer Centre House to the left, with the 1815 Centre House across the side street. This building no longer exists but was still standing at the time of the 1922 auction. (Courtesy of Shaker Museum at South Union.)

SOUTH UNION 1818 MEETING HOUSE. The 1818 Meeting House, located on "the south side of the great road," was one of the early brick buildings at South Union. The first meeting room was located in the 1815 Centre House, where all meetings were held until completion of the new Meeting House. It was used until South Union closed in 1922. The structure was demolished during the 1920s and the bricks used for a dwelling house on the site for the new landowner. (Courtesy of Shaker Museum at South Union.)

SOUTH UNION CENTRE FAMILY SOUTH BUILDINGS. This group of buildings is on the south side of the "great road." The Ministry Shop—home and workshop of the community's elders—is leftmost, then the Meeting House, with the Trustees' Office on the right. The 1824 Centre House is across the street, facing the Meeting House. The railroad crossing, depot, and tavern were down the road beyond the Trustees' Office about one-and-a-half miles. (Courtesy of Shaker Museum at South Union.)

SOUTH UNION 1824 CENTRE HOUSE. This dwelling house replaced the previous Centre House, which was across the road to the east of this building. It measures 60 feet across the front and is 135 feet long. There is a partial basement and two-and-a-half additional stories. Construction began in 1822, and the outside was completed in 1824—the date shown on the front stone—but it was not ready for occupancy until 1833. (Photographs by the author.)

SOUTH UNION CENTRE HOUSE INTERIOR. The photograph above shows the second-floor hall looking north toward the rear of the hall. Note the dual stairways and the beautiful design details. Arches occur throughout the building, especially emphasized in the view of the third-floor hallway below. (Courtesy of Library of Congress, Prints and Photographs Division, HABS [above], and Shaker Museum at South Union [below].)

SOUTH UNION TRUSTEES' OFFICE. The trustees oversaw the business affairs of the society and conducted business with the world from this building. Visitors to the village could also obtain lodging here. The date on the front of the building is 1841, which means the outside was completed during that year. The South Union journal entry for February 8, 1841, reads: "Some brethren & one hireling start to day to get hewn timbers for building a new office—expect to get it some 3 or 4 miles distant near the blacklick creek." An entry on May 12 describes the trip of Jefferson Shannon, who was to travel by horseback to Pittsburgh, Pennsylvania, to purchase nails, glass, and some "Brownish Drab cloth for uniform dress Coats for the Brethren . . . and other articles for the Sisters." En route he was to go through Louisville and pay for joiner work done there and "then visit our friends at U. Village before he goes up the River to Pittsburg." On June 19, "We began to put Tin Roof on our new office today.—Work done by J Jackson and H. L. Eades." (Courtesy of Shaker Museum at South Union.)

SOUTH UNION STREET SCENE. This view of the Centre Family cluster of buildings is looking west. The Centre House is to the right, and the front of the Meeting House can be seen on the left, with a portion of the white Trustees' Office beyond it. Note the sidewalk across the street at the intersection. It is evident that some sisters and brethren posed for this photograph. (Courtesy of Western Reserve Historical Society.)

SOUTH UNION CENTRE SMOKE AND MILK HOUSE. Also called the Preservatory (where the sisters made preserves), it was built in 1835 and is located near the left rear of the Centre House. The left portion of the photograph shows a cow barn built by landowner Oscar Bond in 1936, long after the Shakers left the village. The chimney and roof of the Steam House may be seen in front of the barn. (Courtesy of Shaker Museum at South Union [above]; photograph below by the author.)

SOUTH UNION STEAM HOUSE. This view of the 1847 Steam House looking north shows the cow barn foundation in the background. A journal entry dated October 11, 1847, says, "Building Steam House—Began to build a Small brick Steam house for the cows feed—." (Photograph by the author.)

SOUTH UNION CENTRE WASH HOUSE. Constructed during 1854, the walls consisted of 273,000 bricks, according to a June 15, 1854, journal entry, requiring "8 weeks to a day in building the walls." The photograph below shows the right side and rear of the Wash House, with the adjacent mound cistern used to hold water for use in the Wash House. The rear of the Smoke and Milk House is to the left, and just to the left of it, not in view, is the rear of the Centre House. The small white sign in the foreground shows the former location of the 1849 Ice House. (Courtesy of Shaker Museum at South Union [above]; photograph below by the author.)

SOUTH UNION VIEW FROM BARN SITE. The foundation seen in the foreground is that of the 1919 Shaker cow barn with additions for the 1936 Bond farm cow barn. The Mound Cistern is seen, used to collect and supply rainwater. The 1847 Steam House is nearby. The rear of the Centre House can be seen, with the Well House to its left, and the rear of the Smoke and Milk House to its right. This view is looking south. (Photograph by the author.)

SOUTH UNION OVAL CANDLE STAND. According to Becksvoort (1998), this stand was made around 1815. He provides the following observations: "Made of figured maple, with a beveled oval top, this [is] a very rare South Union stand. (The maple is a northern tree; southern Kentucky furniture usually was made from poplar, cherry, walnut, oak, and hickory.) Barely a decade younger than the founding of the South Union community, the stand obviously was built by an experienced craftsman, who took time to bevel the top and shape a graceful snake foot." (Courtesy of Shaker Museum at South Union.)

SOUTH UNION TRESTLE TABLE. From Becksvoort (1998): "Traditionally, the boards of tabletops run the long way. On this trestle table, as well as four others built at South Union, the top boards run in the short direction—possibly to make thrifty use of short pieces of wood. As a result, this table experiences more than 1 in. of wood movement during the course of an average year. Like many Kentucky pieces, the table is more ornate than its eastern counterparts. There also are structural differences: The braces at the top of each leg support a center rail and two side rails, which form the frame for the eight-board top." The table Becksvoort pictured was made in 1835 of walnut and ash. The one shown here is a rare small "ministry" dining table, made just like the large ones, but for use by two people—either elders or eldresses. (Courtesy of Shaker Museum at South Union.)

SOUTH UNION CHAIRS. These chairs were made at South Union around 1840. The range in size is significant—they are child, youth, and adult chairs from the same period, of the same form and style. (Courtesy of Shaker Museum at South Union.)

Six

BELIEFS AND WORSHIP

The beliefs of the Shakers evolved to some extent over the years, due to the "gifts" of the major leaders and the early lack of codified doctrine. One principle from which they never wavered was celibacy and another was that of communal living and property. Ann Lee and all successive leaders were committed pacifists. Beginning in Ann Lee's time, believers were to confess their sins to a fellow believer. In all aspects of life, believers were expected to submit unquestioningly to their leaders. The worth and equality of every person was another consistent principle of Shaker doctrine and life. Women always held important roles in the society, in starkest contrast with the male domination of the times. The Kentucky societies operated in the midst of slaveholders, leading them occasionally to purchase the freedom of a slave, and to accept converted slaves as equal believers. They required that everyone work with his or her hands, and this applied to the elders and deacons just as it did to all other believers.

Shaker documents were slow in coming, and much that was produced originated in the West. The *Concise Statement of the Only True Church*, written by Joseph Meacham at New Lebanon in 1790, was the first publication endorsed by the society. It was a small brochure that provided a theological framework for Shaker faith and practice. The next significant publication was McNemar's *The Kentucky Revival*, presenting Shaker teaching to those who had participated in the Second Great Awakening but who had "pitched their tents short of mount Zion" (McNemar 1808).

Perhaps the most significant Shaker publication of all time was *The Testimony of Christ's Second Appearing*, written by Benjamin Seth Youngs with assistance from David Darrow and John Meacham. Youngs spent about two years on the large work, completing it in 1808. A second edition contained significant revisions by the New Lebanon ministry (Youngs 1810). In time referred to by some as the "Shaker Bible," it provided a brief history of the movement and presented Shaker doctrine. Most radical was the claim that Ann Lee, along with Jesus Christ, constituted the "two foundation pillars . . . the two anointed ones," and that whereas Jesus revealed the nature of God as Father, Ann Lee demonstrated the nature of God as Mother. Eventually the central ministry made an attempt to recall all copies of the document due to controversy surrounding it. Another publication during this time was John Dunlavy's *Manifesto, or a Declaration of the Doctrines and Practice of the Church of Christ*, written and printed at Pleasant Hill in 1818. Dunlavy took the approach of contemporary theologians in defining and defending Shaker doctrine. As with *the Testimony*, the central ministry was not entirely satisfied with this work. They commissioned two trusted Easterners, Seth Y. Wells and Calvin Green, to prepare a history of the society entitled *A Summary View of the Millennial Church* (Green and Wells 1823). This was the last major publication of the full society.

The worship of the Shakers was highly spontaneous early on, gradually becoming more formalized as customs and rituals developed. Individual families worshiped several times a week in their own meeting rooms, and the entire society assembled in the meetinghouse on Sunday for worship, often followed by another service that was open to the world. Men and women believers entered by separate doors into the meetinghouse and occupied opposite ends of the room. Their worship consisted of dancing, with accompanying songs, and sometimes a sermon or readings from Shaker publications. Attending Shaker worship services was Sunday entertainment for some of their neighbors. On a few occasions when attendees did not behave respectfully, the response was to close worship to the public for a time.

The songs of the Shakers at first made use of a few repeated words or made-up sounds, but by the early 19th century, hymns with words were developed in a style similar to the music of other religious groups of the time. The tune was indicated by use of letters rather than round notes. Many individuals throughout the villages wrote songs. Richard McNemar was especially notable for his contributions, including the hymn "Mother," which appeared in the Shaker song book *Millennial praises* (Millennial Praises 1813). Using the pseudonym Philos Harmoniae, McNemar compiled the 1833 book of Shaker songs entitled *A Selection of Hymns and Poems; for the Use of Believers*. Numerous songs originated in the Kentucky villages—for example, "My Carnal Life I Will Lay Down" originated at South Union in 1838, and "Come Down Shaker-Like" was an early Pleasant Hill song. The best-known Shaker song in our time is "Simple Gifts," composed at Alfred, Maine, in 1848 and incorporated by Aaron Copland into his composition *Appalachian Spring*.

The period from the late 1830s into the 1850s is called the Era of Manifestation, or Mother Ann's Work. The Shakers always believed in spiritual gifts, but this period was especially characterized by spiritual manifestations. The beginning of the period is considered to be August 1837, when 14-year-old Ann Mariah Goff of Watervliet began a series of visions and trances, becoming the spokesperson for messages from Mother Ann. As word spread throughout the villages, similar events occurred. In June 1838, two sisters in the Gathering Order at South Union experienced a trance in which they reported being taken into the spirit world. At Pleasant Hill in September 1838, the first out-of-body experience was reported. The messages and gifts included new songs and dances and "visits" from many foreigners and American Indians. Many of the "instruments" were young, some eventually becoming apostates, which with the strange visions and messages presented a dilemma for the Shaker leaders. The occurrence of the special gifts became less frequent during the 1850s. One notable event during this period was the 1842 edict from New Lebanon that each village was to prepare a sacred site for an outdoor feast to be held twice each year. New Lebanon held their "feast of the passover" in the spring of 1842, and prepared a site that they called "Mount of Olives." Stein (1992) summarizes the rituals at the various sites. The site at Pleasant Hill was called "Holy Sinai's Plain," and the one at South Union was called "The Holy Font of the Lord Jehovah." Locations of these two sites have been determined. The site at Union Village was called "Jehovah's Chosen Square."

The Shakers became well known for the quality and craftsmanship in their work. Yale College president Timothy Dwight (grandson of the famous theologian Jonathan Edwards) visited New Lebanon around 1800, and though he considered their doctrine "silly," expressed admiration for their industry and neatness, ingenuity, and good reputation (Stein 1992). Many of their neighbors admired their workmanship, and the items they manufactured are highly prized by collectors today. Julia Neal (1982) summarized "familiar admonitions, worn smooth by constant repetition," which "became the daily guidelines to true Shakerism":

> INDUSTRY: Do all your work as if you had a thousand years to live and as if you were to die tomorrow.
>
> HONESTY: Be what we seem to be; and seem to be what we really are; don't carry two faces.
>
> THRIFT AND CHARITY: Be prudent and saving . . . so you may have wherewith to give to them that stand in need.
>
> CLEANLINESS: Clean your room well, for good spirits will not live where there is dirt.
>
> ORDER: A place for everything and everything in its place.
>
> HEALTH: Let none abstain from food which they need; eat hearty and do the will of God.
>
> FUNCTIONALISM: That which has in itself the highest use possesses the greatest beauty.

MOSES JOHNSON MEETING HOUSE AT HANCOCK. This meetinghouse is located in the Hancock Shaker Village near Pittsfield, Massachusetts. It is one of the 10 gambrel-roofed meetinghouses designed by Moses Johnson between 1785 and 1794. It was completed in the Shaker village of Shirley, Massachusetts, in 1793 and moved to Hancock in 1962, where it was restored. (Courtesy of Library of Congress, Prints and Photographs Division, HABS.)

NEW LEBANON 1824 MEETING HOUSE. This meetinghouse has a distinctive design, very different than the one it replaced, which was designed by Moses Johnson and served from 1785 to 1824. The large 1824 Meeting House could accommodate 500 worshipers (Stein 1992). Note the three adjacent doors at the left end: the leftmost door was used by the sisters, the rightmost door was used by the brothers, and the center door leads to a stairway to the second floor of the smaller portion of the building, which provided accommodations for the ministry. As was true of all the Shaker meetinghouses, most of the floor was left open for use in the dances. (Courtesy of Library of Congress, Prints and Photographs Division, HABS.)

MEETING HOUSE AT PLEASANT HILL. Sisters are shown crossing the village street to enter the Meeting House. Note that in this later time (late 19th century) men and women are using the same door. The men pictured are non-Shaker visitors who have come to observe a worship service. (Courtesy of the Shaker Village of Pleasant Hill.)

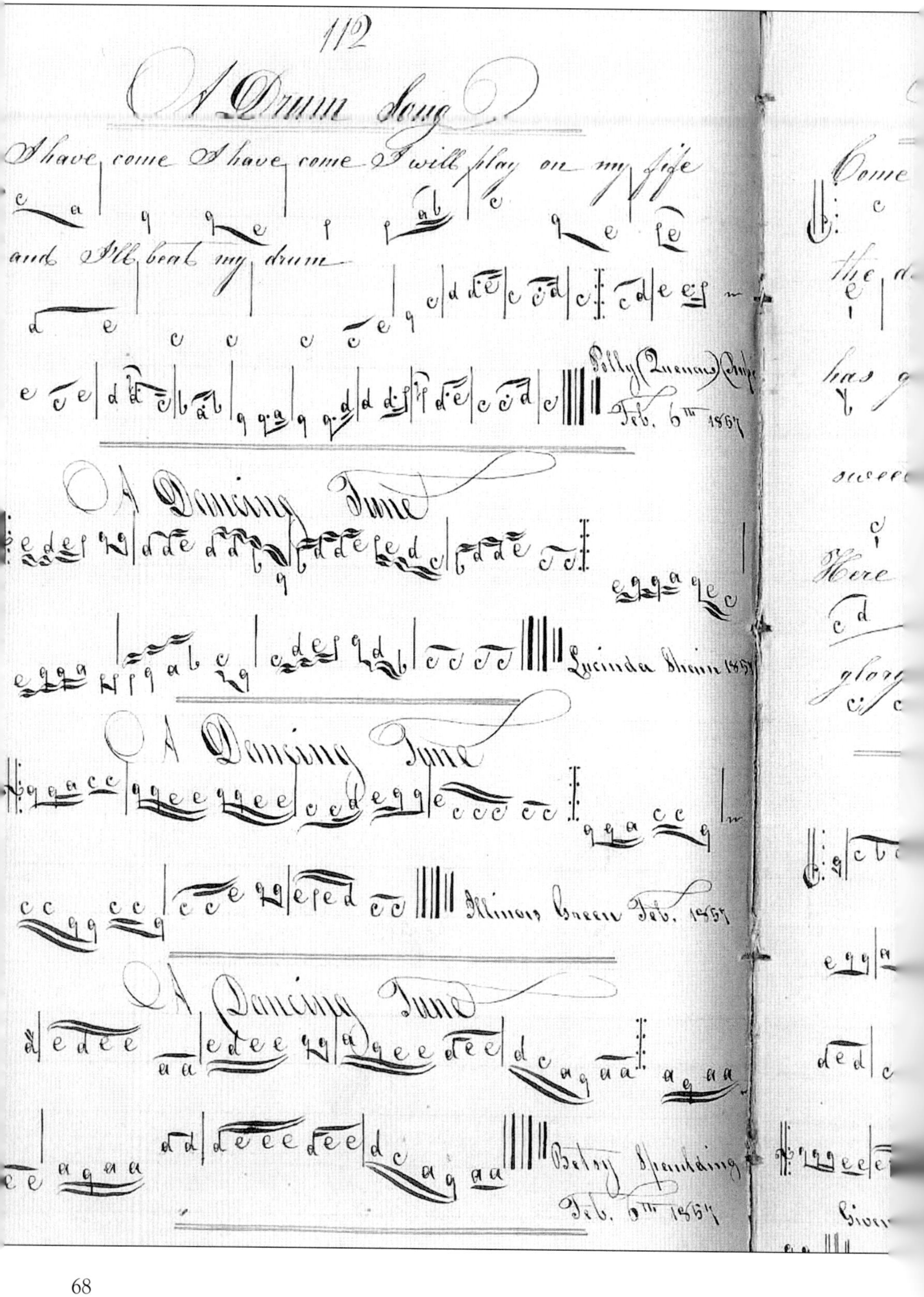

112

A Drum Song

I have come I have come I will play on my fife
and I'll beat my drum

Polly Quenard (?)
Feb. 6th 1867

A Dancing Tune

Lucinda Shinn 1857

A Dancing Tune

Minora Green Feb. 1857

A Dancing Tune

Betsy Spaulding
Feb. 5th 1857

(right column, partial)
Come
the d
has g
swee
Here
d
glory

SHAKER SONGS. This image shows two pages from a manuscript songbook inscribed by Betsy Spaulding in 1903. The compositions are dated between March 1855 and November 1858. Note the innovative use of small letters to reflect the melody and the attribution of a song's source to inspiration from the spirit world. Shaker singing was a cappella, but they had songs whose performance was intended to sound like a musical instrument. "An Instrument Song" is an example of such a song. (Courtesy of the Shaker Village of Pleasant Hill.)

PLEASANT HILL CENTRE HOUSE MEETING ROOM. The Centre Family met daily for worship in their second-floor Meeting Room and worshipped in the Meeting House on Sunday. They learned new songs and dances here and socialized also. (Courtesy of Library of Congress, Prints and Photographs Division, HABS.)

THE WHIRLING GIFT. The drawing depicts an event during the Shaker Era of Manifestations. The sister is represented as having received the whirling gift—the ability to whirl around rapidly in ecstasy during the dance—and has fallen exhausted to the floor (Stein 1992). (Courtesy of www.wikipedia.org.)

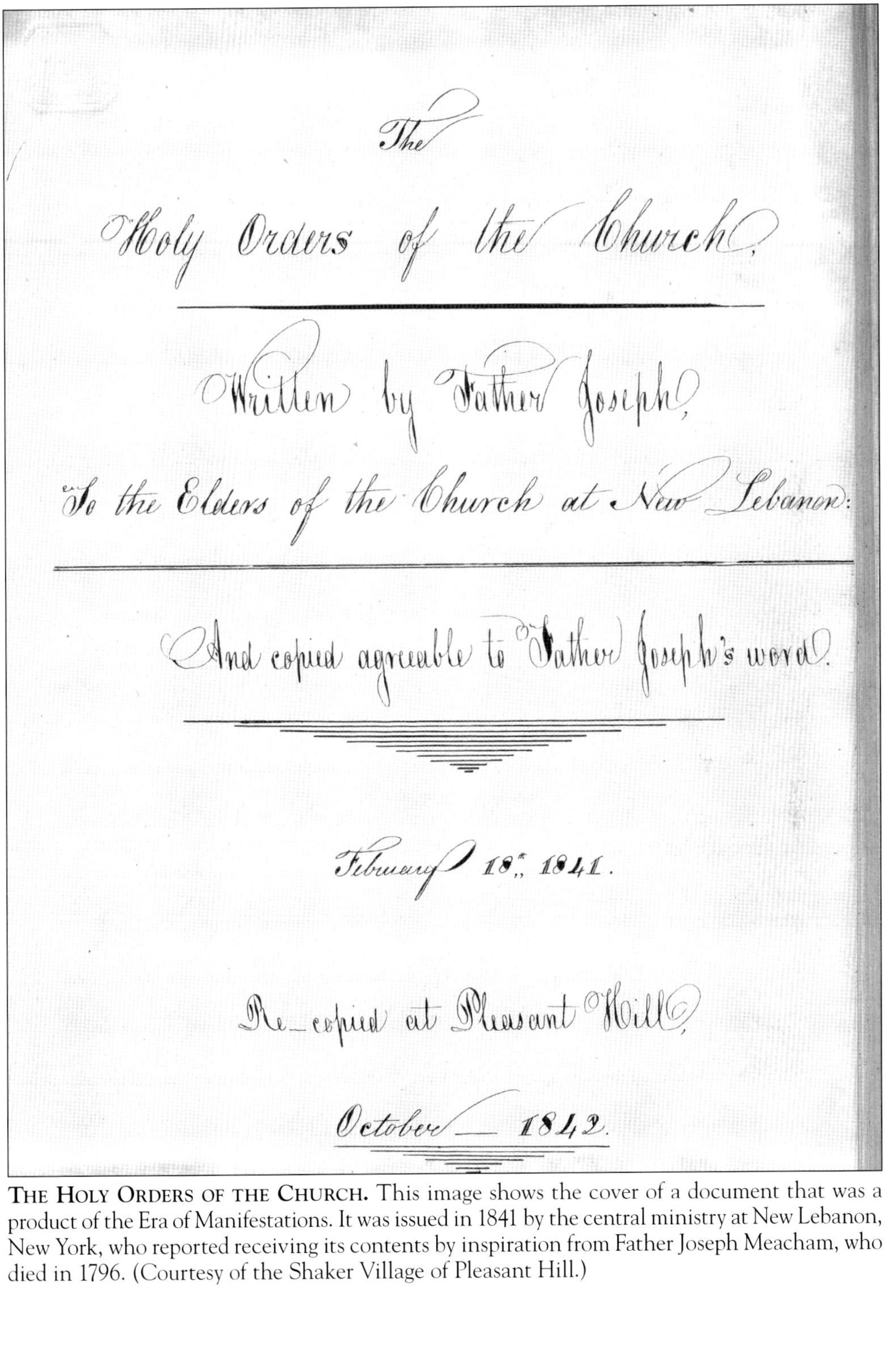

The

Holy Orders of the Church.

Written by Father Joseph,

To the Elders of the Church at New Lebanon:

And copied agreeable to Father Joseph's word.

February 18th, 1841.

Re_copied at Pleasant Hill,

October ___ 1842.

THE HOLY ORDERS OF THE CHURCH. This image shows the cover of a document that was a product of the Era of Manifestations. It was issued in 1841 by the central ministry at New Lebanon, New York, who reported receiving its contents by inspiration from Father Joseph Meacham, who died in 1796. (Courtesy of the Shaker Village of Pleasant Hill.)

July 1st 1832.

Sabbath July

1. _Meetings_ — but poorly attended on acc't of Harvest.

Mon 2 _Demise_ — Good Robert Paisley died of Consumption. He & John McComb who died June 17th 1826 were the only two young men in the Society when the people first believed here — Both lived & died good exemplary Believers. So says Elder Benjamin.

Tues. 3. _Funeral & Burial_ this evening at 5 O'clock.

Wed. 4 _Casualty_ — Wm Roberts stepped on a scythe & cut his foot apparently half off shoe & all! —

Th. 5 _Move_ — Absalom Chisholm Jun'r moved from the Centre & Water & Joseph Roberts from there to the North Family.

Wed. 11 _Building_ — Brick work of N. House Kitchen began by Hirelings — Benj. Perkins Boss —

Sabbath 15 _Shocking! Backsliding!_ This Morning, after breakfast & Singing Meeting was over — Matthew N Houston deliberately left his lot & calling in the Ministry, betrayed his honorable trust & chose a Worldly life — Poor, Man!

Th. 5 _Saving Seeds Sisters_ — Turned out to assist H. L. Eades in saving the Cabbage Seed in the garden while his other hands go to the Wheat Harvest.

Fr. 6. _Wheat Harvest_ — Bro. finished cutting & stooking the wheat — Big days works yesterday & to day — The faithful Sisters — do a part of almost every thing.

SOUTH UNION JOURNAL ENTRIES 1832. The daily activities of life were recorded in the journals at South Union and Pleasant Hill. This journal page contains several entries for July and early August 1832, entries being made only when something worthy of note had occurred. (Courtesy of Shaker Museum at South Union.)

Seven

BUSY LIVES

The Kentucky Shakers, like their brethren and sisters in all the villages, rose from bed early, began specific chores right away, and stayed busy most of the time until bedtime. They had the same household chores to do as any family of the world, but on a larger scale. Much of the work ordinarily done by women of the time was performed by the sisters. The brothers kept wood cut for the stoves and did most of the barnyard chores except milking the cows. The dwelling houses included bedrooms ("retiring rooms") shared by several sisters or several brothers, meeting room, kitchen, dining room, cellar for food storage, and infirmary rooms for care of the sick. Nearby outbuildings included washhouses, smoke houses, well houses, cisterns, and privies. The children of the societies lived together as separate "families" with overseeing guardians, attended school a part of each day, and had assigned duties according to their age and ability, learning to work and helping out with household and farm tasks. The believers worked hard but lived comparatively very well for the time—well housed, clothed, and fed.

Deacons oversaw a family's physical operations, with specific oversight roles for farm, kitchen, orchard, shops, and the like. Observers who visited the villages spoke admiringly of the neatness, orderliness, and good maintenance of the buildings, and the work ethic and cooperation of the believers. The large land holdings of both societies became very productive farms. They grew many crops, including wheat, corn, rye, oats, flax, hemp, potatoes, hay, broomcorn, sorghum cane, sweet potatoes, tobacco, grapes, cherries, apples, peaches, pears, strawberries, and raspberries. Like all the Shaker societies, they were always inclined to try new varieties of plants, farming methods, and implements, and they became known as the best farmers in the region.

The two villages struggled for a few years to provide for their minimal necessities while investing time, effort, and money in developing a support infrastructure to meet their needs over the longer term, and they soon began providing services and products to their neighbors. By 1817, Pleasant Hill "carried on a large stroke of mechanical business," with two gristmills, a sawmill, a clothier's works, a linseed oil mill, a carding machine, six blacksmiths, two tanners, two wagon makers, two wheelwrights, two saddlers, about 10 shoemakers, two ferrymen, two dry measure makers, two reed makers, four coopers, eight or 10 masons, carpenters and joiners, "and 1 hand who makes it his business to make large wooden screws for cider presses, tobacco presses &c." The two gristmills produced $7,000 of flour in 1817 and reported that "the Merchants are always wanting more flour than they can get ground" (Ham 1962).

Services of the fulling mill at South Union were advertised in an 1814 broadside, with agents available in surrounding towns and Nashville where customers could leave cloth and obtain printed instructions "for the information and benefit of Domestic Manufactures in Woolen Cloths." Over 3,200 yards of cloth were on hand to dress when the fulling mill opened in January 1815 (Ham 1962). ("Fulling" is the process of cleansing, shrinking, and thickening cloth by applying moisture, heat, and pressure.) Their flour mills and sawmills also performed services for their neighbors. Among the more unlikely enterprises at South Union was whiskey distilling for the market, which began in 1824 (Neal 1947). Soon thereafter, with direction from New Lebanon, the believers pledged not to use "ardent spirits" in any form. Prior to this edict, all the societies produced wine and cider each year. Within a matter of months, the South Union Shakers were making apple beer.

Beginning about 1830, both of the colonies actively experimented with various breeds of hogs, sheep, and cattle, and their efforts resulted in other farmers in the region becoming interested in Berkshire and Poland-China hogs, Bakewell sheep, and especially shorthorn Durham cattle. In 1847, New Lebanon instructed the believers to end their consumption of pork, but the Kentucky villages continued to raise some hogs. They needed hogs for lard, a staple of the time, and eventually returned to eating pork. In the mid-1830s, New Lebanon provided each Western colony a beginning stock of Bakewell sheep, creating a great deal of interest for a time. But their work with shorthorn cattle had a lasting impact. They bought noted bulls (such as "Shaker" at Pleasant Hill), attended many sales, and imported directly from Europe. South Union purchased cattle from such noted breeders (and citizens) as Henry Clay. Henry Clay also had a business relationship with Pleasant Hill in joint use of a valuable bull. By the mid-1850s, Pleasant Hill and New Lebanon each owned about 450 head of cattle, including more registered shorthorns than any other breeders in America (Ham 1962).

The Kentucky Shaker sisters became widely known for the quality of their preserves (or "sweetmeats")—the two Kentucky societies were the only ones with a commercial enterprise in preserves. The demand in the market was so great that the trustees began to purchase fruit from outside sources. Sometimes they would go to neighbors' fields and pick the purchased fruit (such as strawberries and cherries), and some was delivered to them, including shipments by rail to South Union from as far away as Louisville. The brothers also helped out with the preserves in the busiest times. South Union preserves won the award as the best preserves put up in glass in the United States in the Mechanic and Agricultural Exposition of Louisiana in 1874 (Neal 1982).

The sisters weaved a great variety of products, made cheese, soap, and candles, and also did outside work. They helped with corn husking, gathered seeds for market, cut straw for bonnets and hats, and did the milking. They sometimes prepared meals and took them to the brethren at their work sites. Between 1820 and 1875, both villages had initiatives in silk production. They planted mulberry trees, harvested the leaves, and placed them in silkworm trays for the production of cocoons. The cocoons were placed in hot water, and the sisters then unwound the fibers for spinning. Silk cloth was made into men's collar-width neckerchiefs and handkerchiefs and women's kerchiefs. The sisters also processed straw and wove it into bonnets and hats. For a time, palm leaf was also used for the bonnets and for fans. They also made a large variety of willow and white oak baskets.

Raising and marketing garden seeds was one of the best-known and most profitable industries of the Shakers throughout their societies. They are credited with originating the marketing of seeds in paper packets. They planted fields especially for seed production and grew and marketed different varieties of a given vegetable. They were also very active in production and marketing of brooms.

The lives of the Shakers were not "all work and no play." They sometimes took a playful approach to their work, engaging in "bees" or "frolicks." The sisters competed in "spinning frolicks" and the men in "cornhusking bees" and "grubbing bees," for example. A spinning frolick was held in honor of Eldress Molly's 50th birthday at South Union (Neal 1947). They enjoyed outdoor picnics and sometimes combined them with some work activity or a ride through the countryside. The children also engaged in recreation, such as fishing. Christmas was celebrated, with small gifts exchanged and gifts given to the poor of the world. By the late 19th century, Thanksgiving was celebrated with a large meal and religious activities. Mother Ann's birthday was celebrated on February 29 in leap years, or March 1 otherwise, with readings of Psalms, recitation of poetry, and dances.

PLEASANT HILL FARM FIELDS. This scene from earlier days shows row crops at Pleasant Hill. The societies were pragmatic about their farming endeavors, emphasizing various crops over time depending on the market. Hemp was a major crop in Kentucky prior to 1870, including Pleasant Hill. It was used to make rope and bagging material, including covers for cotton bales. They marketed hemp and made rope for their own use (Clark and Ham 1968). Both societies grew many kinds and varieties of vegetables to generate garden seeds for market, as well as broomcorn and numerous other crops. (Courtesy of the Shaker Village of Pleasant Hill.)

PLEASANT HILL BLACKSMITH SHOP. Each Shaker village had one or more blacksmiths, who met the many needs of each society's homes, shops, and farms and provided for-hire work to neighbors. Pleasant Hill had six blacksmiths in 1817 (Ham 1962). In this photograph, the blacksmith is shown at a forge, which began its use in 1878 near the West Family Dwelling House (Pearson and Neal 1974). (Courtesy of the Shaker Village of Pleasant Hill.)

PLEASANT HILL BROOM FACTORY GROUP. The following information was provided by Larrie Curry of Pleasant Hill. The photograph was made in the late 1880s at the (then) broom shop, built in 1815 as the Carpenter's Shop (now the Craft Sales shop). From left to right in the photograph are (seated) William Tapp (boy—Shaker), Brother John Pilkington (Shaker), and an unidentified female visitor; (standing) Manlius McAndrew (in white, Shaker off-and-on), unidentified man, Lars Ericson (Shaker, in charge of broom industry); two unidentified men, Mary Rochester (in striped dress), who was a frequent visitor from Cincinnati, unidentified man (with pipe), and unidentified female visitor. Of the three unidentified men in the doorway, it is likely two were hired hands and one was a Shaker. Mary Rochester's son was probably the photographer. (Courtesy of the Shaker Village of Pleasant Hill.)

PLEASANT HILL BROOM FACTORY. Broom making occurred in all the Shaker communities beginning first at Watervliet, and it continued to be a profitable endeavor throughout the 19th century. During mid-century, Pleasant Hill had the largest broom trade among all Shaker communities, with six workers making as many as 50,000 brooms during one year and with production above 20,000 during several years. The picture was made in August 1899 and is believed to show Lars Ericson, who oversaw Pleasant Hill broom making. Ericson was a Swedish immigrant and is also seen in the picture above. (Courtesy of the Shaker Village of Pleasant Hill.)

SOUTH UNION 1883 WEST FAMILY DWELLING. This building was constructed after the South Union society had begun to decline, as were the 1867 East Family Dwelling and the 1869 Tavern. This building replaced one destroyed by fire during the Civil War. (Courtesy of Shaker Museum at South Union.)

SOUTH UNION BULL. The Kentucky villages had large numbers of purebred cattle, sheep, and hogs, and were among the most noted livestock authorities and breeders in the country. The brethren attended many sales and imported breeding stock from Europe. (Courtesy of Shaker Museum at South Union.)

SOUTH UNION GROUP BY MEETING HOUSE. A group poses for a picture beside the Meeting House, with a sister observing from the Centre House door across the street. Elder Harvey Eades is at the far right. This warm-weather scene shows the windows open in the Centre House. The picture was made around 1885. (Courtesy of Western Reserve Historical Society.)

Fulling Mill.

THE society called Shakers, in Logan county, Ky. continue their FULLING MILL in operation. Their customers and others living at a distance, are informed, that Cloths, designed to be dressed at their Mill, will be received the present and ensuing season, at the stores of *Amos Edwards*, Russellville—*A. Graham*, Bowling-Green—*S. H. Curd*, Hopkinsville—*J. Tilford*, Nashville—and at the store of *Faulk & Shaifer*, Gallatin—Where also may be had, gratis, printed *instructions*, for the benefit of domestic Manufacturers in woolen cloths.

The precise time for finishing and delivering cloth, cannot be engaged ; but our customers may rely on the utmost punctuality, neatness and dispatch in our power.

N. B. Particular directions, in *writing*, must attend every piece of cloth, stating the owner's name, the county he lives in, the number of yards in each piece of cloth, and what is wished to be done to it. Those directions should also be dated, and *fastened to the inside* of each roll or piece.

No cloths will be received or delivered at our Mill on the *first day of the week*.

JOHN McCOMB, } Agents.
SAML. G. WHYTE, }

South Union, Jasper Spring, Sept. 12th, 1815.

Printed at the Office of the "Weekly Messenger," Russellville.

SOUTH UNION FULLING MILL ADVERTISEMENT. The first conversions at Gasper—later South Union—occurred in 1807. This flyer, dated September 12, 1815, shows that a great deal of progress had occurred in those few years. Promising high quality handling of cloth brought for processing, the flyer states that no transactions may take place at the mill on the first day of the week. (Courtesy of Shaker Museum at South Union.)

78

PLEASANT HILL TOBACCO HARVESTING. Tobacco was grown to some extent in the early years at Pleasant Hill, and beginning in 1914, South Union made arrangements for a tenant farmer to grow it "on the shares" (Neal 1982). The picture was made in September 1912, after Pleasant Hill was officially closed but Shakers were still living there. (Courtesy of the Shaker Village of Pleasant Hill.)

PLEASANT HILL GRISTMILL. This photograph shows the old gristmill abandoned and in disrepair. It began operation in 1817 on Shawnee Run, grinding grain grown in the society's fields for sale on the market. They also ground grain brought in by the world's people. An elevator was used to carry grain to the top floor to move downward through three sets of grinding stones, then back up for two more passes through the stones, and then the meal was ready to pack for the market. The small shed on the right was used when they converted to steam power in the 1880s and tried to revive the milling business (Clark and Ham 1968). (Courtesy of the Shaker Village of Pleasant Hill.)

AN ASSORTMENT OF PEGS. This photograph shows an interesting assortment of pegs made at Pleasant Hill. A visitor to almost any Shaker building will see the omnipresent rows of pegs on the wall. During the early 1870s, after visiting various Shaker communities, Charles Nordhoff wrote, "all the walls, in hall and rooms, are lined with rows of wooden pegs, on which spare chairs, hats, cloaks, bonnets, and shawls are hung; and you presently perceive that neatness, order, and absolute cleanliness rule every where" (Nordhoff 1875). (Courtesy of the Shaker Village of Pleasant Hill.)

BUILT-IN STORAGE. Many rooms in Shaker buildings are outfitted with built-in storage units with shelves and drawers. Good craftsmanship, combined with the vaunted neatness and orderliness of the Shakers, demonstrated the maxim "a place for everything and everything in its place." This storage unit is in the third-floor attic of the Pleasant Hill Centre House. (Courtesy of Library of Congress, Prints and Photographs Division, HABS.)

PLEASANT HILL CENTRE HOUSE KITCHEN. These two photographs, and one on the next page, show different views of the Centre House kitchen, the scene of much activity preparing meals for many sisters and brethren. The items displayed are typical of those that would have been used by the busy sisters. Note the rope from the ceiling in the photograph above, used to ring the bell to call the Shakers in for a meal from their work in shops and fields. The bread oven is seen in the photograph below. (Courtesy of Library of Congress, Prints and Photographs Division, HABS.)

PLEASANT HILL CENTRE HOUSE KITCHEN AND DINING HALL. This view from within the kitchen (above) shows the doorway into the dining hall. The view below shows a portion of the dining hall and the doorway into the kitchen. A visitor said of Pleasant Hill, "In the art of cookery, they excel any people with whom I have been acquainted," and a Cincinnati newspaper stated, "more glorious cookery—I have never met with" (Clark and Ham 1968). (Courtesy of Library of Congress, Prints and Photographs Division, HABS.)

Pleasant Hill Centre House Cellar. The huge cellars under the Centre House provided a great amount of storage space for foodstuffs that benefited from cool, near-constant temperatures, such as potatoes, apples, and molasses. (Courtesy of the Shaker Village of Pleasant Hill.)

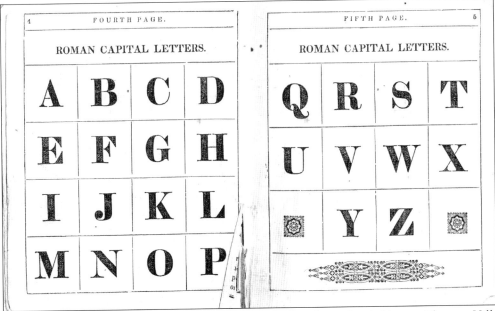

Primer, 1841. Shown is a page from a primer used in teaching the children at Pleasant Hill: *The Common-School Primer: Introductory to S. G. Goodrich's Series of Comprehensive Readers*, published by John P. Morton and Company of Louisville, Kentucky, in 1841. (Courtesy of the Shaker Village of Pleasant Hill.)

ADVICE TO CHILDREN

ON

BEHAVIOUR AT TABLE

FIRST, in the morning, when you rise,
Give thanks to GOD, who well supplies
Our various wants, and gives us food,
Wholesome, nutritious, sweet, and good :
Then to some proper place repair,
And wash your hands and face with care ;
And ne'er the table once disgrace
With dirty hands or dirty face.
When to your meals you have the call,
Promptly attend, both great and small ;
Then kneel and pray, with closed eyes,
That GOD will bless these rich supplies.
When at the table you sit down,
Sit straight and trim, nor laugh nor frown ;
Then let the elder first begin,
And all unite, and follow him.
Of bread, then take a decent piece,
Nor splash about the fat and grease ;
But cut your meat both neat and square,
And take of both an equal share.
Also, of bones you'll take your due,
For bones and meat together grew.
If, from some incapacity,
With fat your stomach don't agree,
Or if you cannot pick a bone,
You'll please to let them both alone.
Potatoes, cabbage, turnip, beet,
And every kind of thing you eat,
Must neatly on your plate be laid,
Before you eat with pliant blade :
Nor ever—'tis an awkward matter,
To eat or sip out of the platter.
If bread and butter be your fare,
Or biscuit, and you find there are
Pieces enough, then take your slice,
And spread it over, thin and nice,
On one side, only ; then you may
Eat in a decent, comely way.
Yet butter you must never spread
On nut-cake, pie, or dier-bread ;
Or bread with milk, or bread with meat,
Butter with these you may not eat.
These things are all the best of food,
And need not butter to be good.
When bread or pie you cut or break,
Touch only what you mean to take ;
And have no prints of fingers seen
On that that's left—nay, if they're clean.

Be careful, when you take a sip
Of liquid, don't extend your lip
So far that one may fairly think
That cup and all you mean to drink.
Then clean your knife—don't lick it, pray ;
It is a nasty, shameful way—
But wipe it on a piece of bread,
Which snugly by your plate is laid.
Thus clean your knife, before you pass
It into plum or apple-sauce,
Or butter, which you must cut nice,
Both square and true as polish'd dice.
Cut not a pickle with a blade
Whose side with grease is overlaid ;
And always take your equal share
Of coarse as well as luscious fare.
Don't pick your teeth, or ears, or nose,
Nor scratch your head, nor tonk your toes ;
Nor belch nor sniff, nor jest nor pun,
Nor have the least of play or fun.
If you're oblig'd to cough or sneeze,
Your handkerchief you'll quickly seize,
And timely shun the foul disgrace
Of splattering either food or face.
Drink neither water, cider, beer,
With greasy lip or mucus tear ;
Nor fill your mouth with food, and then
Drink, lest you blow it out again.
And when you've finish'd your repast,
Clean plate, knife, fork—then, at the last,
Upon your plate lay knife and fork,
And pile your bones of beef and pork :
But if no plate, you may as well
Lay knife and fork both parallel.
Pick up your crumbs, and, where you eat,
Keep all things decent, clean, and neat ;
Then rise, and kneel in thankfulness
To HIM who does your portion bless ;
Then straightly from the table walk,
Nor stop to handle things, nor talk.
If we mean never to offend,
To every gift we must attend,
Respecting meetings, work, or food,
And doing all things as we should.
Thus joy and comfort we shall find,
Love, quietness, and peace of mind ;
Pure heavenly Union will increase,
And every evil work will cease.

From a copy at Shaker Museum, Old Chatham, N.Y.

ADVICE TO CHILDREN ON BEHAVIOUR AT TABLE. This delightful poem consists of a great many rules for Shaker children regarding table manners. It apparently originated at New Lebanon around 1880 and is thought to have been written by Daniel Offord (1843–1911), an elder of the North Family at New Lebanon. It is doubtful that children or adults obeyed all these rules. (Courtesy of the Shaker Museum and Library.)

September 23rd 1852.

This day of september we long shall remember
   This morning we started for pleasure
With our dinner so nice; cakes, custards, & rice
   And other good things without measures.
Before we went out some looked about
   Remarked that the sky was quite hazy.
And prophecied rain again and again
   'Till some almost thought they were crazy.

But nevertheless we gathered our mess
   And rapidly huried away
And little thought we, that such thing could be
   As rain on so happy a day.
We left home at 8 and thought it quite late
   But all seemed perfectly suited;
Our garments were fine, our shoes seemed to shine
   The brethren were were most of them booted

We march'd on our way resolved to play
   In spite of unfavourabl weather
With hearts full of glee we talk merily.
   Both Brethren and Sisters together.

COPYBOOK POEM. This is a poem used as a handwriting model for young students to copy. It was written by Richard Barnett Rupe, who was born in 1829 and came to Pleasant Hill in 1835 with a brother and three sisters when they were all small children. He left in 1853, was gone 13 years, and returned with a wife and child. He left again a couple of years later, with the wife and child remaining. He returned and left several additional times, eventually becoming a physician. His sisters Polly and Nancy were also poets, writing many hymns in their lifetimes. (Courtesy of the Shaker Village of Pleasant Hill.)

Journal of 1856.

Census of the Society. January 1st, 1856.

	First Order	East House	Second Order	North Family	West Lot	Church	Gathering Order	Society
Ministry	4							
Brethren	31	23	21	24	16			
Sisters	60	48	46	29	23			
Total	95	71	67	53	39	233	92	325

January 1, 1856

Tu. 1 The Society at Pleasant Hill, Ky. resumed the use of Col tea and coffee, having abandoned it Oct. 10, 1842. It is only to be used for breakfast at present.

Th. 3 Molly Banta deceased at the Second Order, being 78 years of age the 3rd of last July. She was among the earliest of those who embraced the faith in Kentucky, having set out in Feb. 1806, and has stood through many trying scenes, (where many have fallen,) and has won an imperishable name in the heavens, and is now gone to reap the blessed reward of her faithful labors.

F. 4 Mercury 2° below 0.— On the 5th at 15 above 0—On the 6th at 10°.

M. 7 Mercury at 30°. Snowed most of the day, making about 4 inches in depth with some that had previously fallen.

Tu. 8 Mercury at 2° above 0.

W. 9 Mercury at 17° below zero in the morning, and never rose higher than one degree below zero during the day— at 9 P.M. it was 8 below again. On the 19th of January 1852 it was 15° below zero in the morning, & never got higher than 2° below 0 during the day, & on the morning of the 20th of the same it was 18° below In Feb. 1835 it was 18 below one morning, and in some places it was 20° below the same morning.

PLEASANT HILL JOURNAL, JANUARY 1856. Exhibiting beautiful penmanship, the writer began the year by carefully recording the census by family. The total of 325 is down from the high of 490 in the early 1820s. A tribute was written in remembrance of Molly Banta, a member of one of the founding families at Pleasant Hill. (Courtesy of the Shaker Village of Pleasant Hill.)

Eight

INTERACTION WITH THE WORLD

In order to enjoy the economic prosperity the Shakers desired, and ultimately achieved, interaction with non-Shakers was necessary. Most of their villages, including those in Kentucky, were situated along public roads. Pleasant Hill owned a ferry site on the Kentucky River nearby, and South Union had the Louisville and Nashville (L&N) Railroad running through its lands, with a depot and a small hotel situated along the tracks. Many visitors came their way, including Pres. James Monroe, Gen. Andrew Jackson, and traveling companions at South Union in 1819. The believers were delighted to welcome such highly placed visitors but turned no one away.

In 1812, the Kentucky legislature passed a law permitting the granting of a divorce when either a husband or wife joined the Shakers. The spouse not joining was to be awarded property and custody of all minor children. At South Union for example, after William Boler became a convert in 1808, his wife, Sally, brought suit seeking possession of their land and custody of their son. Before the decision was rendered, William Boler deeded the land to the society and took their son, Daniel, to New York, where he grew up to become an elder in the central ministry at New Lebanon (Neal 1982). Occasional threatening incidents occurred when backers of a disgruntled parent sought to remove children from the Shakers.

Throughout Shaker history, there were instances of believers returning to the world as "backsliders," including even a few prominent leaders. In April 1828, after a turbulent period of leadership struggles, Samuel Banta seceded from the society at Pleasant Hill, which was built partially on land he had provided. Banta and a fellow dissenter brought suit to reclaim their property. Richard McNemar came from Union Village to help Pleasant Hill in its defense. The case was dismissed in 1831. Banta appealed to the Kentucky Court of Appeals, which ruled in favor of the society, citing the Shaker covenant signed by believers and taking the position that the court had no right to intervene in an internal religious struggle.

Marketing activities of the Shakers were extensive, varying by village. Local trade occurred from the Trustees' Office of each village. The closest cities for the regional trade were Nashville, Louisville, and Lexington, but their range extended to St. Louis, Memphis, and Vicksburg and towns along the river routes to New Orleans. Pleasant Hill began river journeys on flatboats at their own Shaker Ferry nearby on the Kentucky River, while the river portion of South Union's trips began either on the Red River or the Cumberland River. In late October, they would begin the annual journey to New Orleans, transporting garden seeds, various manufactured products, and livestock. After conducting their sales, the brethren would buy a year's supply of items needed by their village, such as sugar, coffee, tea, molasses, rum, dried fish, tanner's oil, glass, and iron, returning to South Union or Pleasant Hill in late January or February. The Shaker traders traveled in pairs and were constantly reminded that, though they were of necessity in the world, they were not of it. The societies aggressively advertised their merchandise, sold on credit, gave discounts on large orders and cash, placed goods on consignment, and threatened legal action for nonpayment. The Shakers earned a reputation in all their markets for good quality at a fair price (Ham 1962).

From the days of Joseph Meacham, the Shakers saw no virtue in unnecessary labor, and this attitude helped them achieve the level of productivity they enjoyed in farming and other activities. They kept up with new labor-saving inventions and bought the best equipment available on the market. For example, the water supply system at Pleasant Hill is thought to have been the first successful municipal water system in Kentucky. They made improvements to inventions of others and made many inventions of their own. In the early days, the Shakers were opposed to patenting their inventions, thinking it inconsistent with their principles. However, after having some of their inventions patented by others, and even facing the prospect of having to pay royalties to someone else to use an invention of their own, they began to obtain patents. Following are patents known to have been obtained by Kentucky Shakers—Pleasant Hill: truss for hernia, 1836; improvement in cartridges, 1856; and improvement in dumping wagons, 1876; South Union: washing machine and churn, 1831; plough, 1861; grain separator, 1866; combined seeder and cultivator, 1866; and double shovel plow, 1867 (Richmond 1977, Hooper 2003).

The War of 1812 caused some difficulties for the Shakers. Young Shaker men were sent draft notices, and while some served, military duty was in opposition to Shaker pacifist principles. A ruling by the Kentucky Court of Appeals upheld the Shakers' right to refuse military service based on their beliefs. This brush with war paled in comparison to the issues the Civil War would bring. As a border state, Kentucky's role in the North-South conflict was complicated. After a political struggle, the legislature voted to keep Kentucky in the Union, and the state militia went to the Confederate side. Bowling Green, near South Union, was chosen as the Confederate capital and the location of heavy contingents of Confederate troops. The road passing through the village was the state route connecting Bowling Green and Russellville, so there was constant movement of troops. Most of South Union's neighbors were Confederate sympathizers, whereas most of Pleasant Hill's neighbors were Union loyalists. The issue of conscription of Shaker young men for military service became an issue. Following an appeal from the South Union ministry to President Lincoln in 1863, Secretary of War Edwin Stanton telegraphed the "Provost Marshall of Bowling Green," directing that conscientious objectors should be released from service.

The Kentucky Shakers found themselves at odds with the Confederate adherents because of their stand on slavery and suspect by those on the federal side because of their pacifist stand. Principle and strategy led them to show courtesy to both sides. During the war years 1861 to 1864, there were many instances of both Confederate and federal troops passing through the villages or camping nearby, and placing demands on the villages for horses, wagons, feed for horses, clothing, firewood, and especially demands for food for the hungry men. Their journals reflect their compassion for the frequently hungry, bedraggled soldiers coming to their villages, and they never denied them food. They fed huge numbers of soldiers at a time—as many as 1,000 in a day—and the sisters sometimes got up in the middle of night to cook for them. They devised various strategies to keep from giving up their horses and to protect their dwelling houses. They kept lookouts at night and sometimes hid their horses far from the village.

The Confederate retreat from Kentucky in October 1862 marked the end of major battles in the state, but skirmishes and guerrilla activity would continue through 1864. The war years were very disruptive to the lives of the believers at Pleasant Hill and South Union, as to their neighbors. They were unable to continue their trade routes during the war and were never able to fully restore them. Though peace was restored to the villages, the vibrancy that characterized them before the war was never to be regained.

KENTUCKY 1830 STATE HOUSE.
Kentucky's "Old State House" or
"Old Capitol" served as Kentucky's
capitol building from 1830 to 1910,
when the current capitol building was
completed. During a brief occupation
of Frankfort by Confederate troops in
October 1862, this building was the
scene of an inauguration ceremony to
install Richard Hawes as "Provisional
Governor" of Kentucky. The ceremony
was interrupted by federal troops who
drove the Confederates out and re-
installed the Stars and Stripes on the
dome of the building. The photograph
below shows the rotunda. The
building has served as the home of the
Kentucky Historical Society since 1920.
(Historical notes and images courtesy
of Library of Congress, Prints and
Photographs Division, HABS.)

ADVERTISING BROADSIDES FROM PLEASANT HILL. These advertisements reflect the aggressive marketing strategies employed by Kentucky Shakers. Such products as Elixir of Malt were popular remedies of the time. The broadside above provides an address at Pleasant Hill, whereas the one below reflects use of an agent in Louisville to extend marketing opportunities. (Courtesy of the Shaker Village of Pleasant Hill.)

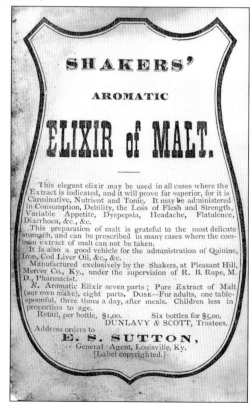

90

FERRY AT SHAKER LANDING. These photographs show the ferry at Pleasant Hill's Shaker Landing on the Kentucky River, about two miles from the village. The picture of a ferry arriving was made in the late 1880s, and the picture of the departing ferry was made in the late 1890s or early 20th century. Pleasant Hill is in Mercer County, and the opposite riverbank is in Jessamine County. This was one of several landings used by Pleasant Hill in the 19th century, but this one became the principal shipping point. It was the beginning and ending point for many marketing trips made by the Pleasant Hill brethren to New Orleans and to numerous towns along the river route. The "High Bridge" was built nearby, which ended the need for the ferry, although the usefulness of the landing site remained. (Courtesy of the Shaker Village of Pleasant Hill.)

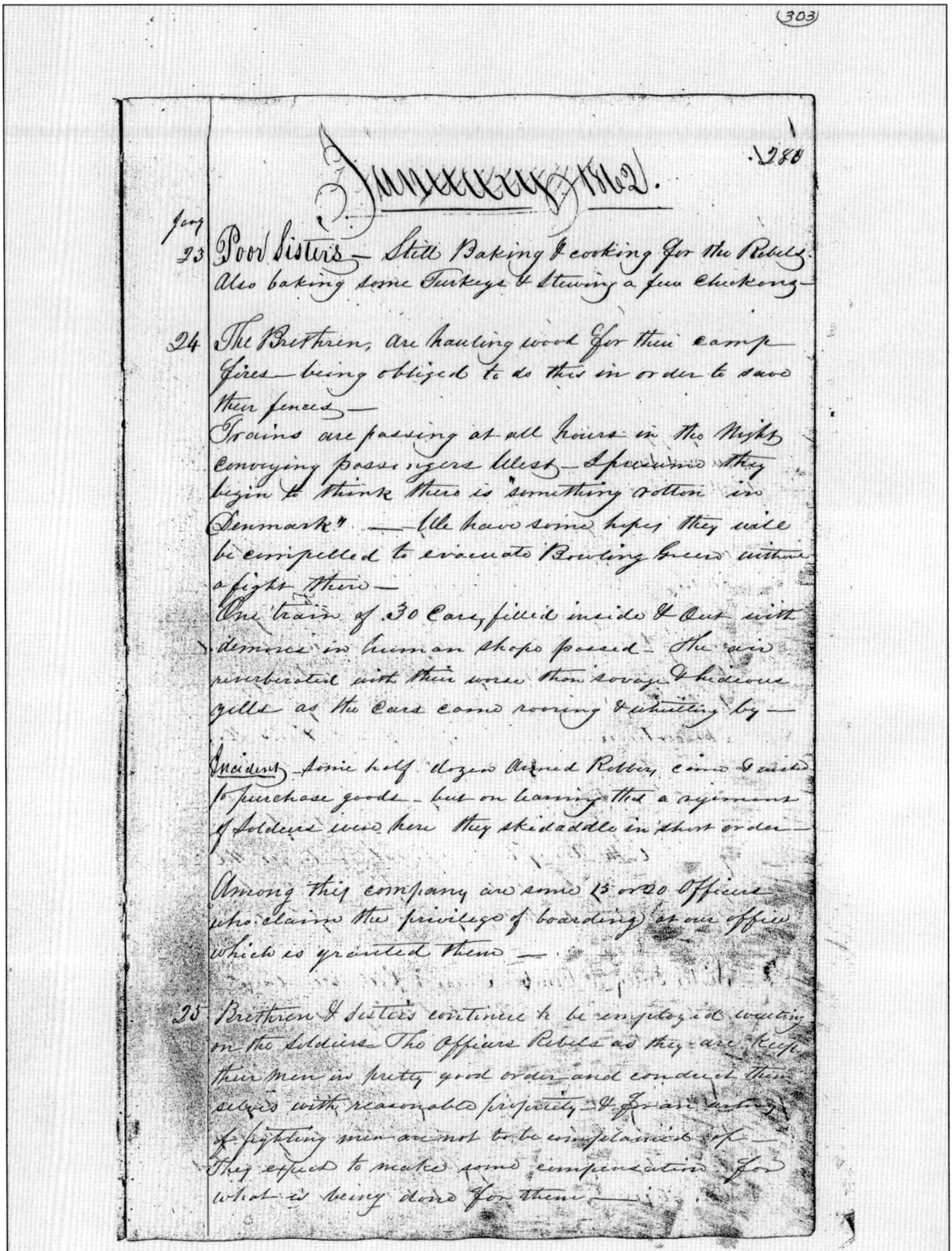

[Handwritten journal page dated January 1862, page 288]

January 1862.

23 Poor Sisters — Still Baking & cooking for the Rebels. Also baking some Turkeys & stewing a few Chickens —

24 The Brethren, are hauling wood for their camp fires — being obliged to do this in order to save their fences —
Trains are passing at all hours in the Night conveying passengers West — I presume they begin to think there is "something rotten in Denmark." — We have some hopes they will be compelled to evacuate Bowling Green without a fight there —
One train of 30 Cars, filled inside & out with demons in human shape passed — The air reverberated with their worse than savage & hideous yells as the Cars came roaring & whistling by —

Incident, Some half dozen Armed Robbers, came & asked to purchase goods — but on learning that a regiment of Soldiers were here they skedaddled in short order —

Among this company are some 15 or 20 Officers who claim the privilege of boarding at our office which is granted them —

25 Brethren & Sisters continue to be employed waiting on the Soldiers. Tho' Officers Rebels as they are keep their men in pretty good order and conduct themselves with reasonable propriety, & a more orderly set of fighting men are not to be complained of — They expect to make some compensation for what is being done for them —

SOUTH UNION JOURNAL CIVIL WAR ENTRIES. This is a page from the South Union Journal, dated January 1862. The January 23 entry states, "Poor Sisters—Still Baking & cooking for the Rebels." On the 24th, brethren were hauling firewood to the troops to keep their fence rails from being burned. "Trains are passing at all hours in the night" loaded with troops, "savage & hideous yells as the cars came roaring & whistling by." Officers were boarding at the Trustees' Office. (Courtesy of Shaker Museum at South Union.)

12 village, in sight of the North Family, to prevent surprise. How awful to think of a wicked and bloody battle occurring in the midst of Zion on earth; those in the village placed a strong guard at the cross roads by the Carpenter shop, and occupied the road back to the North Family, and pickets, guards and couriers patroled the streets and road towards Harrodsburg till one o'clock P.M. when General Morgan ordered them to move up the road apiece, and not disturb the tranquility of our people any longer. Gen. Morgan and his staff then came up and took dinner, and returned again towards the river. In about an hour those on the road towards Harrodsburg returned and reported 30 thousand Federals, moving on from Harrodsburg towards this place, and they skedaddled towards Nicholasville. This, however was in part a false alarm, not quite so many. While they were dining, and frequently through the day (Sabbath) the booming of cannon could be distinctly heard, proclaiming in tones of thunder, the work of death and destruction between those beings that call themselves the offspring of God, created in his image and likeness, and now the demons of blood and carnage! During the transit of the multitudes yesterday and the occupancy of the village to day, no depredations were committed upon our persons or property, strict orders being given by the officers to abstain from all aggressions, which were rigidly enforced, and we were treated with all due respect and politeness. General Morgan himself setting example. In the evening when the sun disappeared, the fires at Camp Dick Robinson, about 6 or 8 miles distant air line, towards the South east, and the Federal camps southward, forming part of a circle toward the South West, could be seen from this village, illuminating the horizon like the aurora borealis of the north. A perfect calm prevailed around our borders, while the hostile hordes around this jovial camp fires, within three or four miles of each other, were supplying the cravings of hunger and thirst, hundreds not knowing that they would ever see another sun go down. Strange events! Whoever would have thought that this secluded and sacred spot of holy Pleasant Hill would

PLEASANT HILL JOURNAL CIVIL WAR ENTRIES. This entire journal page discusses the stay of Confederate general J. H. Morgan and his troops at Pleasant Hill a few days after the Battle of Perryville, which was fought on October 8, 1862. It was the largest Civil War battle fought in the state of Kentucky. Perryville was less than 20 miles from Pleasant Hill. After brief stops in the area, Morgan retreated through the Cumberland Gap into East Tennessee, with the Confederate offensive now ended in Kentucky and the Union controlling the state. (Courtesy of the Shaker Village of Pleasant Hill.)

POULTRY!

After many years experience with the popular varieties of Poultry, we are convinced that for the farmer, as well as the amateur fancier, the BRAMA AND PATRIDGE COCHINS are the *best known varieties*. We are therefore giving particular attention to

THE IMPROVED LIGHT

Bramas and Partridge Cochins Fowls

which have attained to a state of perfection and excellence superior to any known breed of Fowls, produced by a close personal attention given to selection and crossing on the best stock of Fowls to be had.

Price, per Pair.

Light Bramas,	$5 00
Partridge Cochins,	5 00

Price, per Trio.
[Two Hens and a Cock.]

Light Bramas,	$7 00
Partridye Cochins,	7 00

Eggs carefully packed in dry saw dust and delivered to express companies at $2 00 per dozen.

☞Address Orders to

JANE COWAN,
South Union, Ky.

December, 1876.

SOUTH UNION POULTRY ADVERTISEMENT. This broadside touts Brama and Partridge Cochins for sale, "superior to any known breed of Fowls." Eggs are offered, packed in dry sawdust. Eldress Jane Cowan oversaw South Union's poultry business for many years. (Courtesy of Shaker Museum at South Union.)

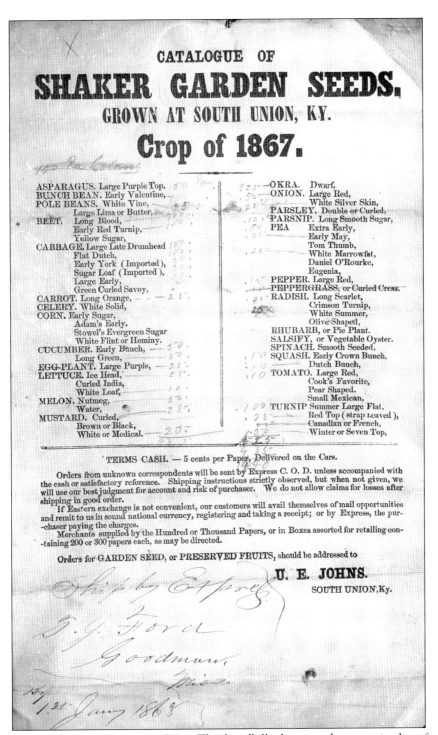

SOUTH UNION GARDEN SEEDS FOR SALE. This handbill advertises the extensive list of garden seeds from the 1867 crop. Someone has handwritten the cost per packet and an address in Goodman, Mississippi, for express shipment. The contact is shown as U. E. Johns (Urban), who was a trustee. (Courtesy of Shaker Museum at South Union.)

Surveyed for William Brown and Joseph
Ficklin a certain tract or parcel of land, situate, on
Shawnee run,
lying and being in the county of Mercer and state
of Kentucky, and bounded as follows, to wit; beginning
in Cave's original line and adjoining the settlement
and preemption of Henry Prather, at a stone, corner
to a tract of land conveyed by Robt. Denny to David Denny and which is included in this survey as part of it,
and running thence N. 75¾ E. 10.17 chains to another stone
known as no. 60 in the possessing of the land belonging
to the Shakers; Thence N. 1 W. 24.75 ch. to another stone
corner to Tomlinson and Shakers, marked 61; Thence S. 59°
W. 22.20 ch. to a stone in Cave's line aforesaid, and corner to Tomlinson, formerly Robt. Denny's North west corner; Thence with sd Cave's line S. 31¼ E. 2.46 ch to a
white Oak corner to Tomlinson; Thence with Tomlinson's line S. 38½ W. 10.05 ch. to a stone, oposite to a large
white oak in sd line; Thence S. 39½ E. 35.33 ch to a
stone in a line of W. 76. Taylor Dec.; Thence with his
line N. 51½ E. 4.20 ch, to a stone in the line aforesaid
of Richd Cave; Thence with sd. line N. 31¼ W. 17.27 ch.
to the beginning — Containing 57 A. 3 R. & 20 poles.
Pleasant Hill Ky.
14th August 1845.   Micajah Burnett.

LAND SURVEY BY MICAJAH BURNETT. This is a copy of a land survey performed by the talented Burnett. He signed and dated it on August 14, 1845. He was about 54 years of age at the time. (Courtesy of the Shaker Village of Pleasant Hill.)

Nine

DIFFICULTIES AND DECLINE

The 1850s was a good time economically for the two societies. Clark and Ham (1968) referred to this period as the "golden decade" for Pleasant Hill. The appraised value of the Pleasant Hill farms increased from $96,000 to $170,000 during the decade. The usual approach of the societies was to invest extra money in land, and during this decade, Pleasant Hill spent $50,000 for more land. South Union bought several additional farms, loaned more than $20,000 to other societies, and began buying L&N Railroad and county bonds. But the cost of running the societies was great. They provided a lifestyle for all their residents that was comparatively luxurious for the time. They educated the children at their own expense—with the majority of the youth leaving before they could make a productive contribution. They took care of their own elderly, paid a large amount of tax on their lands, helped out other societies in distress, and were generous to the poor of the world.

The Reconstruction period after the war was a time of trouble and uncertainty for the villages, including thefts by outsiders and issues with their own young people. At South Union in 1871, a disgruntled young sister set a fire in the attic of the Centre House, which fortunately was extinguished, but evidence of the fire can be seen today. A group of Swedes were brought to Pleasant Hill to help with the shortage of manpower, and in 1873, the son of one of their leaders set fire to the north lot cow barn, completely destroying it and its contents. The Civil War exacerbated problems that had already begun to occur. The increasing industrialization in America diminished the usefulness of the Shaker mills and made obsolete various services and products they had earlier provided. They turned to farm-based enterprises to a greater extent than previously, and especially so after the Civil War, emphasizing garden seeds, herbs, broom making, and preserves. Among the Western societies, South Union and Pleasant Hill had the greatest emphasis on farming and were the most prosperous during this time. South Union had the largest seed trade of the Western villages. The number of packets ("papers") sold was 32,290 in 1831, increasing to 175,000 in 1852 with revenue of about $7,000. Pleasant Hill had income from seed of about $4,500 per year during the decade of the 1850s. Seed was typically marketed as boxes of 150 or 300 packets. Pleasant Hill had the largest broom trade among all Shaker societies, with six workers producing 50,000 brooms by 1850, with a value of $8,330. Broom making continued to be profitable for most of the century, after seeds and preserves were no longer profitable. The percentage of men versus women in the societies had been steadily declining. The sisters assumed increasingly important roles in the enterprises, while the need for farm labor led the societies to hire non-Shaker men to complement their own workers. The New Lebanon ministry warned that this practice was opening "a door or sluiceway of destruction, especially for the rising generation" (Ham 1962).

The trend of diminishing spiritual and economic health was evident in the bad decisions and malfeasance of some of the leaders. At the Western oversight village of Union Village, the lead elder, John Martin, was removed from office in 1858 after going against the advice of the trustees and taking the society into debt. In the same year, the lead elder at North Union—near Cleveland—left the society, leaving it $2,400 in debt. Giles B. Avery, an elder in the central ministry at New Lebanon, visited the Ohio communities in 1862; he wrote that he found a "great lull of interest & energy to maintain the gift of God" and observed that "favorable circumstances in life are not the great securities of success. . . . mankind can bear prosperity only in proportion to their development in virtue and goodness" (Ham 1962).

All the Shaker villages were experiencing decline in population during this time, with the average age of residents increasing. The climate of religious fervor that gave rise to the Great Awakening, the Second Great Awakening, and Shaker beginnings was long past, and adult converts were rare. The very nature of Shaker doctrine and lifestyle was no longer attractive to an increasingly worldly minded people. Difficult economic times no doubt led some of the earlier converts to come to the villages with their children, but industrialization had increased opportunities elsewhere. The villages lost many of their younger and middle-aged men to the lure of lives and opportunities in the world. One approach tried by many of the villages was to accept orphans with the hope they would become Shakers, but a very small percentage remained until mature adulthood. Along with the increase in age came a decline in effective leadership, as aged leaders served after their abilities were greatly diminished, frequently compounding difficult situations with bad financial decisions. There was a gradual decrease in worship emphasis and an increase in social activities and amusements. During the declining years of the societies, they began furnishing their rooms in the style of their neighbors of the world and acquired such modern conveniences as indoor plumbing and telephones. In 1915, South Union purchased a new Reo automobile.

In 1880, Pleasant Hill had 203 members and South Union 99, then in 1900, they had 34 and 55 respectively (Stein 1992). By 1910, Pleasant Hill indebtedness had resulted in much of the property being sold. In that year, with 12 Shakers remaining, an agreement was made to deed the remaining 1,800 acres to nearby resident George Bohon, who was to care for the remaining 12 Shakers. The last two to die were Dr. William Pennebaker in 1922 and sister Mary Settles in 1923. South Union continued until 1922, and from 1917, when Union Village closed, until 1922, it was the only remaining Western village. In 1922, when South Union property was sold at auction, there were two men and seven women remaining. They were offered the choice of relocating to New Lebanon or receiving $10,000 each. Elder Logan Johns opted to relocate to New Lebanon, and Josie Bridges, who was deemed mentally incompetent, was also taken to New Lebanon. Two of the nine, Lizzie Simmons and William Bates, married. Annie Farmer and her mother, Alice Mason, moved to Louisville. Annie Farmer died in 1942, the last of the Kentucky Shakers.

Shaker population reached its peak in the 1820s, with estimates of over 4,000 members at all villages (Stein 1992), down to 2,415 in 1874 (Nordhoff 1875). Stein (1992) estimates the 1880 total as 1,849 and the 1900 total as 855, then 516 in 1906, 367 in 1916, 192 in 1926, 92 in 1936, and 40 in 1951. In 1947, New Lebanon, New York, closed, followed by Hancock, Massachusetts, in 1960. Canterbury, New Hampshire, closed with the death of the final member there in 1992. This leaves only Sabbathday Lake, Maine, where today there are four Shakers, ranging in age from the 40s to the upper 70s. It is remarkable that, against major odds, the Shakers were so successful for so long. They have been the most successful and enduring communal religious organization in the history of America.

Fortunately the villages of Pleasant Hill and South Union are now open to the public and are providing an opportunity for thousands of visitors each year to understand the beliefs, lives, and contributions of the people who lived there.

PLEASANT HILL SISTERS AT OLD FULLING MILL. The Shakers occasionally took a break from work to go for a walk in the countryside or go on a picnic. In this photograph, two Shaker sisters and two visitors are seen along the stream beside the old fulling mill. The picture below was made on the same day, with the two visitors appearing in both pictures. (Courtesy of the Shaker Village of Pleasant Hill.)

PLEASANT HILL SHAKERS AND VISITORS WITH A PHOTOGRAPHER. A group observes the work of a photographer at the Kentucky River Palisades. The woman at left is a Shaker, as are the two men at the right, one of whom is thought to be Francis Pennebaker. The three other people are thought to be members of the Montgomery Rochester family of Cincinnati, frequent visitors during the 1880s. Shaker Landing and the nearby High Bridge attracted a great deal of interest on the part of travelers. A number of vintage postcards of the late 19th century show scenes in this area. (Courtesy of the Shaker Village of Pleasant Hill.)

ELDER HARVEY EADES. Eades was born in 1807, shortly before his parents joined the South Union community, and spent all his life in the society. At age 29, he was appointed to leadership at South Union, second to Benjamin S. Youngs. He became well known within the Shaker communities. In 1844, he was reassigned to Union Village, Ohio, where he served in various roles before returning to South Union at the beginning of the Civil War. He then served in leadership in Kentucky until his death at age 84, serving for a time in a joint oversight role for both Pleasant Hill and South Union. His autograph can be seen on the picture below. (Courtesy of Western Reserve Historical Society [above] and Shaker Museum at South Union [below].)

Elder Harvey Eades   NEW GROUND FLOOR STUDIO,
UPPER MAIN STREET,
BOWLING GREEN, KY

HARVEY EADES'S ACTIVITIES. Eades's first name sometimes is seen as "Hervey," and his last name was sometimes spelled "Eads." Though educated only within the society, he wrote and spoke well and is considered by some to have been the most able advocate of a conservative doctrinal position within the entire society during his time (Andrews 1963). He wrote a number of Shaker songs. This picture appeared in a book he wrote in 1879 entitled *Shaker Sermons: Scripto-Rational*. He was required to justify the seeming vanity of including his picture (Stein 1992). (Courtesy of Shaker Museum at South Union.)

SOUTH UNION 1869 TAVERN. Built as a business venture, the small hotel accommodated travelers of the world. It was built along the newly completed L&N railroad about one-and-a-half miles from the Shaker village. The photograph shows the corner of the railroad depot to the right. The society bought the brick in Bowling Green and the furniture in Cincinnati. From the beginning, the Tavern was run under a lease arrangement, first by a Mr. Wethered, who was to pay the society $1,200 per year (Neal 1947). The Tavern operated until the village closed in 1922 and now serves as a bed and breakfast operated by the Shaker Museum at South Union. (Courtesy of Canterbury Shaker Village.)

SOUTH UNION GROUP IN 1885. The picture was taken on the lawn behind the Meeting House. The women in the first row have been identified as, from left to right, Elvarine Hilton, Charity Hilton, unidentified, Sabrina Whitmore, Eldress Betsy Smith, two unidentified, and Eldress Nancy Moore. The woman in the second row is unidentified. The only man identified is Elder Harvey Eades, second row center. (Courtesy of Western Reserve Historical Society.)

SOUTH UNION 1917 STORE. This old store building is across the road from the Tavern, and like the Tavern, it was operated under a lease arrangement. Originally there was a frame building on the site, which was replaced in 1872 by a brick building. Fires in 1884 and 1896 resulted in two replacement structures being built. At one time, a post office was also operated in the back of the store. (Courtesy of Shaker Museum at South Union.)

OLD HIGH BRIDGE VIEWED NEAR SHAKER LANDING. The so-called High Bridge opened in 1877, carrying the Cincinnati Southern Railway across the Kentucky River. It was 275 feet tall and 1,125 feet long and was dedicated by Pres. Rutherford B. Hayes in 1879. It is said to have been at that time the highest bridge in North America and the highest railroad bridge in the world. The railroad diminished the importance of the Shaker Landing and ferry to some extent. Given the beautiful setting of the bridge above the river gorge, the area became a tourist attraction. Pleasant Hill capitalized on the opportunity by taking in boarders and running a taxi service to the ferry and to the north end of the bridge (Clark and Ham 1968). The large covered boat was likely an excursion boat. (Courtesy of the Shaker Village of Pleasant Hill.)

PLEASANT HILL TRUSTEES' OFFICE AS GUEST HOUSE. In 1896, Gen. John B. Castleman of Louisville bought 766 acres of Shaker land and the Trustees' Office for just over $20,000. The Trustees' Office subsequently served as the Shaker Village Guest House (shown) and operated as a restaurant during the mid-20th century prior to restoration of the village (Clark and Ham 1968). (Courtesy of the Shaker Village of Pleasant Hill.)

CHANGING VIEWS AND PRACTICES. Over time, significant changes took place in Shaker dwelling houses, reflecting changing views and practices. Spare furnishings were giving way to personal and decorative touches and different styles of furniture. The photograph above shows a bedroom at Pleasant Hill, likely in the East Family house when in use as Shakertown Inn. The spinning wheel is from an earlier time, while the ornate bed and pictures are very different than before. The photograph below was taken around 1900, with the building uncertain. It shows what is believed to be a late Shaker retiring room. Curtains are now in use at the windows, and numerous decorative items have been acquired. Two beds are visible in this room, one of them in the foreground. (Courtesy of the Shaker Village of Pleasant Hill.)

THE PENNEBAKER BROTHERS. Brothers William and Francis Pennebaker were brought to the West family at Pleasant Hill as orphans following the cholera epidemic of 1849, and they would remain there all their lives. The society arranged for them to be educated, with William becoming a physician and Francis becoming a dentist. Under the influence of William Pennebaker, who was dissatisfied with the leadership and society direction of Elder Benjamin Dunlavy, the West Family withdrew from the oversight of the society in 1878, followed shortly by the East Family. The properties and assets of these families were separated from those of the society. With the community already in decline, this added to the problems faced by the aging leadership (Clark and Ham 1968). William is shown in the carte-de-visite photograph above, made about 1880. Francis is shown below (center) with a group, perhaps at Mackinaw Island, Michigan, where he spent weeks at a time due to asthma. (Courtesy of the Shaker Village of Pleasant Hill.)

THE PENNEBAKERS AND CHANGING TIMES. The photograph above shows Drs. William (far left) and Francis Pennebaker (standing by his side) with others. They both wore clothing in the style of the time rather than the traditional styles of Shaker men. William is shown below at the West Family House entrance. Note the decorative plants and shrubs, very different from the earlier days in the village. William died in 1922, leaving only Mary Settles as a surviving member of the Pleasant Hill society (Neal 1982). (Courtesy of the Shaker Village of Pleasant Hill.)

PENNEBAKER INITIATIVES. After becoming independent from the Pleasant Hill society, the West Family was led by Dr. William Pennebaker. He and his brother, Francis, engaged in various enterprises, generally prospering financially. They leased land, raised livestock, and even invested in racehorses—one of which is shown. They invented a "dumping wagon" and jointly patented it. The picture of girls at the West Family House was made after William Pennebaker's death in 1922, when the Pennebaker Home for Girls operated there (Neal 1982). (Courtesy of the Shaker Village of Pleasant Hill.)

WILLIAM PENNEBAKER WITH A GROUP OF SISTERS. This photograph, likely made in 1879, shows Pleasant Hill West Family leader William Pennebaker posing with a group of sisters. Standing from left to right are Sarah Pennebaker, Mary Constant, William Pennebaker, and Cynthia Shain. It is known that Betsy Spaulding is on the front row, perhaps on the far right. The others are not identified. (Courtesy of the Shaker Village of Pleasant Hill.)

ELDERLY SISTERS AT PLEASANT HILL. The increasing dilemma of all the Shaker communities is represented by this fascinating photograph of four elderly sisters in front of the Centre Family dwelling. Sister Mary Settles is on the far right, and probably Sister Susan Shain Murray is on the left. During the latter part of the 19th century, the average age in the Shaker communities steadily increased, as did the percentage of women to men. Very few new converts were coming in, and many younger and middle-aged men were leaving for lives and opportunities in the world. (Courtesy of the Shaker Village of Pleasant Hill.)

SISTER MARY SETTLES. Pleasant Hill officially closed in 1910, with the property deeded to a local businessman who cared for the 12 remaining elderly Shakers until their deaths. In 1912, only three remained at the Centre House—Mary Settles, Susan Murray, and Sarah Nagle. In 1923, when Mary Settles died, she was the last remaining Pleasant Hill Shaker. Note that in the first picture she does not wear the traditional bonnet. This was just one of many indications of changing views and emphasis within the Shaker communities. (Courtesy of the Shaker Village of Pleasant Hill.)

This Cut represents our 2 Horse or 50 Bushel

IMPROVED DUMPING WAGON,

------FOR------

COAL, BRICK, GARBAGE, Etc.

------MANUFACTURED BY------

PENNEBAKER BROTHERS,

PATENTEES,

PLEASANT HILL, KENTUCKY.

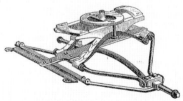

Improved Platform Front Gear, Patented July 10, 1882.

Our Front Gear is constructed mostly of iron. The Springs are mounted on iron bars forming an arch, by means of which we secure great strength with moderate weight. This part of our invention is adapted to general use in platform work.

Satisfaction Guaranteed,

PENNEBAKER BROTHERS.

PENNEBAKER DUMPING WAGON. This broadside shows an 1882 patent date. Prototypes were built, but very few of the wagons were ever sold. (Courtesy of the Shaker Village of Pleasant Hill.)

SISTER JANE SUTTON AND SHAKERTOWN INN.
By 1896, fewer than 60 Shakers were left at
Pleasant Hill, and buildings were beginning to
show neglect. The Trustees' Office and a large
tract of land were sold in that year. Also that year,
a businessman from Lexington opened a hotel in
the East Family House (called the Shakertown
Inn) and placed Sister Jane Sutton in charge. A
guest is shown leaving the Shakertown Inn (Clark
and Ham 1968). (Courtesy of the Shaker Village
of Pleasant Hill.)

SHAKERTOWN INN DINING ROOM. Shown is the dining room in the Shakertown Inn. The furniture gives little evidence of Shaker influence, and the wallpaper and decorative touches are indicative of the time. The pegs along the walls are a reminder that this was a Shaker dwelling. (Courtesy of the Shaker Village of Pleasant Hill.)

SISTER SUSAN SHAIN MURRAY. Sister Susan oversaw the raising of poultry at Pleasant Hill. Prior to her death, she became one of only three surviving Centre House residents (Neal 1982). (Courtesy of the Shaker Village of Pleasant Hill.)

JAMES SHELTON, PLEASANT HILL MILLER. James Shelton was active at Pleasant Hill during its declining years. When he died in 1910, his funeral was conducted by the minister of the Christian church of Harrodsburg, with singing by their choir. As early as 1894, a neighboring minister had conducted a funeral in the Pleasant Hill Meeting House. By this time, worship in the various Shaker communities was in decline. Pleasant Hill stopped dancing in worship after 1885, and at South Union, very few religious services were held after 1900 (Stein 1992). (Courtesy of the Shaker Village of Pleasant Hill.)

CYNTHIA AND HER DUCKS. Despite the decrepit state of the properties, life goes on. Sister Cynthia Shain is seen feeding her ducks, with a few chickens joining in. (Courtesy of the Shaker Village of Pleasant Hill.)

SHAKERTOWN BAPTIST CHURCH. Between 1910, when Pleasant Hill closed, and 1966, when restoration began, the village buildings had various uses. This sign shows the use made of the Meeting House for a period of time. It was also used for a time as an automobile repair garage—which attests to its sturdiness. (Courtesy of the Shaker Village of Pleasant Hill.)

PLEASANT HILL WATER HOUSE DETERIORATING. During the years from 1910 to 1961, the Pleasant Hill buildings were under various ownerships and uses; some were in an advanced state of deterioration, and some were removed. Fortunately restoration began soon enough (1966) to save the major buildings and many smaller ones (such as this one) as well. (Courtesy of the Shaker Village of Pleasant Hill.)

TRI-COUNTY MEDICAL SOCIETY 1911 MEETING AT SOUTH UNION. The participants in this meeting, from the Kentucky counties of Logan, Warren, and Simpson, posed with a few South Union residents on the west lawn of the Centre House, with the Meeting House visible across the road. Shaker John Perryman is on the left end, kneeling, Sister Josie Thrall is the third person from the left in the same row, and Sister Sabrina Whitmore is fourth from left. During the previous year, Pleasant Hill had officially closed, and South Union would hold on until 1922. (Courtesy of Shaker Museum at South Union.)

JAMES CARR OF SOUTH UNION. The one-time owner of this photograph made sure the subject would be known. Carr was at South Union during the time of significant decline. He wrote a letter in 1895 that was published in the Shaker *Manifesto* journal, suggesting a remedy to the problems in Kentucky. "We are with a full supply of muscular energy, a force which is very useful in many an occupation," he wrote, suggesting that Eastern Shakers come to Kentucky where they would find a "more genial climate & fertile soil" and could "blend their mental culture with our muscular energy" (Neal 1947). By that time, the Eastern Shaker villages were in decline as well, and Carr's hopes were not to be realized. (Courtesy of Shaker Museum at South Union.)

SHAKER JOHN PERRYMAN OF SOUTH UNION. These photographs were likely taken around the same time as the 1911 Medical Society photograph, in which John Perryman also appears. He was listed in a journal entry dated August 24, 1862, as being part of the Centre Family and 18 years of age. On March 5, 1863, "John Perryman moves from the Centre to the North to take charge of the boys—". On April 26, 1864, "Sheep-Shearing—The brethren of the different families commenced shearing the Sheep to day. . . . in all 700 head Logan Johns, J. Perryman & one or two others sheared 50 head each to day—". The women in the above photograph are visitors. (Courtesy of Shaker Museum at South Union.)

CHANGING TIMES AT SOUTH UNION. A car passes the Centre House, one among many changes that came to the old village. In April 1915, South Union's elder, Logan Johns, purchased a new Reo automobile for the society. An employee of the Bowling Green car dealer spent a day at South Union teaching William Bates to drive. Subsequent journal entries report that they "went for a ride in auto after supper tonight" and took visitors for a ride—"They think it is just fine." An October 1915 journal entry recorded that "Fourteen automobiles passed here this afternoon going west through Auburn" (Neal 1947). (Courtesy Shaker Museum at South Union.)

SOUTH UNION FURNITURE AUCTION. This broadside advertises an auction of Shaker furniture in April 1922. Furniture auctions began at South Union in 1920, and this was the last significant furniture sale before the September 1922 auction of the land and buildings. (Courtesy Shaker Museum at South Union.)

LAST CALL!
FOR
ANTIQUE FURNITURE
AT
SHAKERTOWN, KY.
(RAILROAD STATION, SOUTH UNION, KY.)

Sat. April 8, 1922
BEGINNING AT 10:30 O'CLOCK A. M.

The Shaker's real estate and live stock having been sold, we will sell with outreserve or by-bid, beginning at 10:30 A. M., all of the household and kitchen furniture made and used by the Shakers, consisting of Chest of Drawers, Tables, large and small, Twin Beds, Wardrobes, Cupboards, Straightback Chairs, Feather Beds, Carpets and Bed Clothes, and other articles too numerous to mention, which were made by the old time Shakers from

Solid Walnut, Cherry AND Oak

Practically all of this furniture is in good condition and much of it is more than 100 years old.

This is absolutely the best furniture that has been offered for sale at any of the auctions and will positively be your last chance to buy antique furniture made by the Shakers in Logan County at your own price. For after April 8, Shakertown will be a thing of the past. We want you to come to this sale. Get off at South Union Railroad Station, where you will have free transportation to and from sale. TERMS CASH.

FREE—OLD TIME BARBECUE

Will sell rain or shine and in case you do not attend sale, J. W. Wallace, South Union, Ky., or Col. W. A. Holeman, Russellville, Ky., will handle mail bids with care.

United Society of Shakers

COL. W. A. HOLEMAN, Auctioneer, Russellville, Kentucky
Place Shakertown, Ky.   Time 10:30 A. M.   Date Saturday, April 8th., 1922

SOUTH UNION AUCTION. The auction sale of the South Union property was held September 26–27, 1922. The first photograph shows a few people arriving for the sale, walking east, with the 1810 Building on their left and the Trustees' Office to their right. The second picture shows the huge crowd assembled in front of the Centre House. The old 1815 Centre House can be seen at the right side of the picture. (Courtesy of Shaker Museum at South Union.)

ACTIVITY AT SOUTH UNION AUCTION. The degree of interest in this auction sale is reflected in these photographs. In the first picture foreground, a table is visible holding food for sale prepared by local churchwomen. It is evident from this picture that this was a social event for many attendees. The second photograph shows the auctioneers in action. Farm machinery, cattle, Shaker furniture, and books were auctioned. The auction at South Union resulted in the land and buildings being bought by an investment company. After sale of the timber on the property, the land was subdivided and sold as multiple properties (Neal 1947). (Courtesy of Shaker Museum at South Union.)

BOND FARM PANORAMIC VIEW. Oscar S. Bond was a member of the investment company that bought all the South Union land and buildings at auction. When it was later subdivided, he purchased a large tract containing the buildings and operated a farm there for many years. He removed the Meeting House and built a home on the site—which may be seen in this picture. The photographer was on the front steps of the Centre House. (Courtesy Shaker Museum at South Union.)

SOUTH UNION 1810 BUILDING IN 1929. A note on the back of this picture lists the date as July 21, 1929. That is seven years after the auction sale. Apparently this historic old building was allowed to decay to the point that it was removed. (Courtesy Shaker Museum at South Union.)

SOUTH UNION WASH HOUSE IN DECLINE. This picture of the Wash House shows a lack of maintenance, with missing and deteriorating shutters. A closer look would justify the handwritten comment on the back of the picture, "Better brick or better walls are not to be found in the Green River Territory." The note is thought to be a quote from a 19th century journal or letter. (Courtesy of Shaker Museum at South Union.)

SOUTH UNION CENTRE PERSPECTIVE. This photograph was taken from the walk between the 1880 Mound Cistern and the Smoke and Milk House, looking south along the side of the Centre House. A part of the Meeting House can be seen across the street from the Centre House, and the white-painted Trustees' House, also across the street, can be seen to the right. The small structure over the 1830 Well can be seen to the left of the row of trees. The grounds show signs of neglect. (Courtesy of the Shaker Museum at South Union.)

SOUTH UNION CENTRE HOUSE AS HOME TO BENEDICTINE MONASTERY. The picture above shows the Centre House during the time it was used by St. Maur's Monastery and Seminary of the Roman Catholic Order of St. Benedict, which began at South Union in 1947. The Centre House and acreage with it were purchased for a Shaker museum in 1971. The recent picture below shows the entrance to the Roman Catholic Fathers of Mercy operation, which is housed in the old Centre Family Wash House. (Courtesy of Shaker Museum at South Union [above]; photograph below by the author.)

PLEASANT HILL CARPENTER SHOP AS A GENERAL STORE. The first photograph was made in 1940. This is another example of the use made of buildings between village closing and the beginning of restoration. Built in 1815 as the Carpenter's Shop, it was later used as the Broom Shop. The building serves today as a craft sales shop, shown in the second picture after restoration. (Courtesy of the Shaker Village of Pleasant Hill.)

PLEASANT HILL GRAVEYARD. This vintage photograph shows the Pleasant Hill cemetery overgrown, with no believers left to revere the memory of those who were eulogized and buried here over the years. Fortunately this cemetery has been restored and is maintained today. Someone has written initials on two tombstones in this photograph, but the identity of the individuals buried there is not known. Sadly the limestone tombstones at South Union were removed by the landowner after the property auction, ground up, and used as lime on the fields. (Courtesy of the Shaker Village of Pleasant Hill.)

REMEMBERING JULIA NEAL. Mary Julia Neal (1905–1995) was a native of Auburn, Kentucky, growing up with the South Union Shakers as neighbors. She became widely known as a Shaker scholar and author (including three books listed in the bibliography section). She earned undergraduate and graduate degrees from Western Kentucky University (WKU) and taught English for some years—including a number of years at Florence State University, where the author knew her first as a teacher and then briefly as a colleague. She returned to WKU in 1964 and served until 1972 as director of the Kentucky Museum and Library. She spent the rest of her life dedicated to the development of the Shaker Museum at South Union, serving from 1972 to 1980 as voluntary codirector with her childhood friend Deedy Hall. In advance of her death, she arranged for the "daily guidelines to true Shakerism" (provided in chapter six) to be read at her funeral. Tommy Hines, her protégé and admirer, wrote in a tribute to her, "Her love for Kentucky, for Logan County, and for the Shakers will leave a lasting impact on those who knew her and on generations to come." (Courtesy of Shaker Museum at South Union.)

Ten

PLEASANT HILL AND SOUTH UNION TODAY

The Shaker Village of Pleasant Hill and the Shaker Museum at South Union are today operated as nonprofit corporations preserving the heritage of the historic villages and hosting thousands of visitors each year.

Restoration of Pleasant Hill began in 1966, following more than 50 years of private ownership and varying uses of the land and buildings. U.S. Highway 68 was rerouted in order to restore the village road to its 19th-century appearance. Restoration has been achieved for 34 historic buildings, which are surrounded by more than 2,900 acres of the original land. Pleasant Hill is the largest of all restored Shaker communities and is one of the premiere historical preservations in America. Pleasant Hill was the first historic site to be designated in its entirety as a National Historic Landmark. Visitors may take advantage of overnight lodging in historic buildings, enjoy food prepared from Shaker recipes at the Trustees' Office, tour the buildings and property, and benefit from interpreters in period costumes. Numerous special events and workshops are held at the village each year. The sternwheeler *Dixie Belle* provides excursions from nearby Shaker Landing. A great deal of information about the village is available online at www.shakervillageky. org. Arrangements for a visit may be made through the Web site or by calling 800-734-5611.

Following the closing of South Union, a large tract containing the buildings was operated as a farm for many years by O. S. Bond. He removed the Meeting House and built a home on the site. Subsequently the property was owned and used by the Benedictine order. The Centre House and several other buildings were purchased from the Benedictines in 1971, with state assistance, to establish a Shaker museum. Numerous restoration projects have been completed, and others continue. The Shaker Museum at South Union operates from the Centre House, where extensive original furnishings and artifacts depict the lives of the believers and interpreters add to the visitor's experience. The museum owns 500 acres of the original land, along with seven original buildings. Visitors may take advantage of accommodations in the Shaker Tavern, which is operated by the museum as a bed and breakfast. Additional information may be obtained by consulting the Web site www.shakermuseum.com, or by calling 800-811-8379.

CURRENT SCENES AT PLEASANT HILL.
The excursion sternwheeler *Dixie Belle* passes the point where the Dix River flows into the Kentucky River, with High Bridge and Shaker Landing nearby. Broom making demonstrations are provided in the East Family Brethren's Shop. Historic farming interpreters are shown moving hay along the village road in the West Family area. (Courtesy of the Shaker Village at Pleasant Hill.)

CURRENT SCENES AT SOUTH UNION. A Centre House exhibit presents a period room from around 1890, when the Shaker interiors were very much like anyone else's home. Everything in the exhibit was actually used at South Union. An interior view of the Smoke House meat room is seen, where meat was cut before it was hung in the smoke room above. The room is on the first level of the Smoke and Milk House on the Smoke House side. (Courtesy of Shaker Museum at South Union.)

BIBLIOGRAPHY

Andrews, Edward Deming. *The People Called Shakers.* New York: Dover Publications, 1963.

Becksvoort, Christian. *The Shaker Legacy.* Newtown, CT: The Taunton Press, 1998.

Brewer, Priscilla J. *Shaker Communities, Shaker Lives.* Hanover, NH: University Press of New England, 1986.

Clark, Thomas D. and F. Gerald Ham. *Pleasant Hill and Its Shakers.* Harrodsburg, KY: Pleasant Hill Press, 1968.

Conkin, Paul K. *Cane Ridge: America's Pentecost.* Madison: The University of Wisconsin Press, 1990.

Green, Calvin and Seth Y. Wells. *A Summary View of the Millennial Church.* Albany, NY: Packard and Van Benthuysen, 1823. (2nd ed. 1848.)

Ham, F. Gerald. "Shakerism in the Old West." (Ph.D. Diss., University of Kentucky). Ann Arbor, MI: University Microfilms, 1962.

Hooper, James W. "Innovation in the Former Shaker Communities: Principles for Present-Day Application." Paper presented at the 12th International Conference on Management of Technology, Nancy, France, May 2003.

http://www.passtheword.org/SHAKER-MANUSCRIPTS/Millennial-Church/millndex.htm

McNemar, Richard. *The Kentucky Revival.* Cincinnati: E. and E. Hosford, 1808.

Millennial Praises: Containing a Collection of Gospel Hymns in Four Parts Adapted to the Day of Christ's Second Appearing. Pittsfield, MA: Hancock, 1813.

Neal, Julia. *By Their Fruits: The Story of Shakerism in South Union, Kentucky.* Chapel Hill: The University of North Carolina Press, 1947.

———. *The Kentucky Shakers.* Lexington, KY: The University Press of Kentucky, 1982.

Nordhoff, C. "The Shakers." *The Communistic Societies of the United States.* (Republished, with new introduction, in 1966). New York: Dover Publications, 1875.

Pearson, Elmer R. and Julia Neal. *The Shaker Image.* Boston: New York Graphic Society, 1974.

Richmond, Mary L. *Shaker Literature: A Bibliography.* Hanover, NH: University Press of New England, 1977.

Stein, Stephen J. *The Shaker Experience in America: A History of the United Society of Believers.* New Haven: Yale University Press, 1992.

Stone, Barton W. "The Biography of Elder Barton Warren Stone, Written by Himself; with Additions and Reflections by Elder John Rogers." Paris, KY: The Cane Ridge Preservation Project, 1847. Republished in *The Cane Ridge Reader.* Ed. by Hoke S. Dickinson, 1972.

Youngs, Benjamin Seth. *The Testimony of Christ's Second Appearing.* 2nd ed. Albany, NY: Hasford, 1810.